Late Harvest Green

**An Idaho Farm Family
Through
The 20th Century**

Late Harvest Green
An Idaho Farm Family Through The 20th Century
By Lois Requist
All Rights Reserved
Copyright 2018
Published by Benicia Literary Arts
Benicia, California
www.benicialiteraryarts.org
www.loisrequist.com
www.lateharvestgreen.com

ISBN 978-0-9703737-8-6
Library of Congress Control Number: 2018942689

Editor-in-Chief, Mary Eichbauer
Editors: Sherry Sheehan, Ann Kurteff, and Linda Foley
Cover painting by Susan Street, susanstreetartist.com
Cover photography and design by Thomas Eric Stanton
Interior Layout by Lois Requist
Family Tree by Carrie Requist

Published by Benicia Literary Arts, which encourages reading and writing in the community by producing events, creating a community of writers and readers, encouraging their development, and publishing works of high quality in all genres.

Also by
Lois Requist

Where Lilacs Bloom
First Edition, 2000

RVING SOLO ACROSS AMERICA
...without a cat, dog, man, or gun
2009

Where Lilacs Bloom
Second Edition, 2017

Table of Contents

1955

1970

1997

Johnson Family Tree

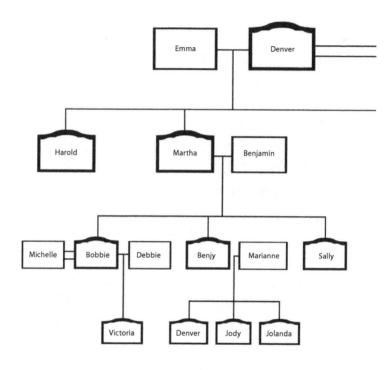

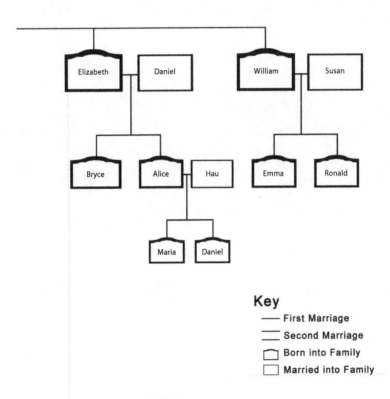

Noreen

Elizabeth — Daniel

William — Susan

Bryce

Alice — Hau

Emma

Ronald

Maria

Daniel

Key
— First Marriage
= Second Marriage
⬡ Born into Family
▢ Married into Family

Chapter One

1955

His life, an empty plate. What would he do with the rest of it? At forty-seven, sitting in a café drinking coffee in Kuna, Idaho, Denver Johnson wondered this as he looked down at the stub of his missing finger. He thought about many things once a part of his life that were now gone, especially his wife, Emma, whose death a few months earlier had caused a numbness in him, a lack of reason or purpose.

Her absence reminded him of all that was past— his youth, his dreams, the energy surging through him as a boy while singing Christmas carols in the snow. That resonance had carried as if the sound might travel forever, blanketing the earth and welling up within him.

He was unaware that Noreen, the waitress, observed him from the other side of the counter through a display of frosted cakes and homemade pies. She could almost feel the cloud of dejection that surrounded him. Clearly, he wanted to be alone to ride out his grief.

Pushing a strand of blonde hair behind her ear, she picked up the steaming pot of coffee and approached him, interrupting his thoughts. "Some more coffee, Mr. Johnson?"

She held the pot, poised to pour. He could see the pink uniform and her lively brown eyes on him and that ever-so-quick glance at his right hand, where a finger was missing.

"'Bout half, Noreen." With his left hand, Denver pushed the heavy white mug across the counter, barely looking up, but aware of the extra attention she'd paid him since his wife died.

She turned away. He tried to slip back into his own thoughts, unable, however, to erase Noreen completely from his mind. She'd noticed the space where his second finger should be, something he never talked about.

A missing digit, a stub instead of an arm or part of a leg vanished, such sights were fairly common. He'd seen men return — the lucky ones — from two world wars, with some part of them buried in Bataan, along the Normandy coast, or in the dirt of other European or Pacific battlefields. Men frequently suffered accidents while farming also. Earning their living with their bodies, they put hand to plow, saw to wood, and back to loading bales of hay. Toiling through each long day, the men helped animals give birth, moved dirt and stone, manipulating their world to earn a livelihood.

Denver thought that, for Noreen, the story of his absent finger might fill a void, a need for excitement that the town of Kuna did not provide. 'Course, men were always thinking some part of them necessary to fulfill a woman.

The daily activity of the café continued. He nodded at familiar faces without encouraging further exchange. He had the scene memorized. Red counter stools. Gray Formica-and-chrome tables and chairs hugging the opposite wall, each with its brightly lit jukebox so customers could spend a nickel, choose a song, and hear the music.

The face of the cook popped up regularly from the kitchen opening, calling out something unintelligible to all, but Noreen and the other servers responded by carrying steaming plates of bacon and eggs, chicken fried steak, or meat loaf with mashed potatoes and gravy to waiting patrons.

Noreen tore a check from her thick pad and put it upside down on the counter in front of Denver.

"Are you keepin' things up inside the house since . . ." she let the thought dangle. "Do you need any help? Aw—I see there's a button missing here." She gestured toward the left cuff of his worn and dirty denim jacket.

"No, well, I'm doin' the best I can," he said, absently running his fingers across his stubbled chin and through his thinning hair. Of average height with a slight build, he'd been called puny by his brothers.

Today, he wore tattered Levis and a plaid shirt. It'd been awhile since these clothes had seen the inside of a washing machine. A smear of manure was visible on one pant leg.

"Looks like spring is coming on. I guess your busy time's about here." She waited while he pulled out his wallet.

"I s'pose." He was aware of her interest in him, and not entirely averse to it. Still, he'd been paralyzed by Emma's death and was still in a quagmire of his own that didn't allow him to respond.

"I could help, you know. On my day off—I could give the place a real good scrubbing."

He felt a flush rising along the neck of his shirt. "That might be all right. I'll think about it."

"I'm off on Mondays. I could come over next week. What time would work? After breakfast? Or, I could come up and fix you some breakfast, and then go to work." She spoke loud enough for him to hear, but softly, so as not to get the attention of other diners.

He pictured her bringing her womanly body into his house. Probably in her early forties, she wore short blondish hair—what people often referred to as dishwater blonde—brushed back to reveal her widow's peak. Makeup brought some color to her thin face. A spot of rouge on each cheek stood out like a marigold in brown earth. She exuded energy, or hope, or some indication of purpose that he'd forgotten about or lost. He didn't know whether he could stand her presence in his house. He shuddered at the imagined intrusion.

"Don't worry, Mr. Johnson. I won't touch anything you want left alone."

He started toward the door without answering her.

"Next Monday. About eight, then?"

He cleared his throat and nodded.

"See you Monday, Denver." Over his shoulder, he caught her bright smile.

Cowboy boots clomping through the morning air, he walked toward his mud-splattered pickup. He got in slowly, and tried to turn on the motor. After a couple of failures, it coughed and held a rough rumble.

He drove home in the early waking of spring. Most of the snow from a late winter storm was gone. The ground showed stirrings of life. Tufts of green poked out of the soil. Here and there, in a low spot where the sun didn't reach, a snowdrift clung, stubbornly glowing, icy at its edges.

He turned off the main road onto the dirt lane that led to his home. The path was rutted, the holes soft and damp. He swerved and wended his way carefully to avoid becoming stuck between the high center and low muddy spots.

He saw a piece of fallen fence in his field. The barbed wire had slipped into a limp and awkward position. Two uprooted wooden posts lay almost flat. To the right, his neighbor's property was lined with tall trees, now barren and brown. Branches stretched up and out against the gray sky. Running alongside the trees was a straight, sturdy fence, erected just two years ago.

In contrast to his place, this order, strength, and purpose struck him like a shot of glaring light illuminating the futility of his life. He felt alienated from the vital universe around him. Not a sharp break, this separation, but a gradual dissolution of the elements inside that once connected him to the earth.

Chapter Two

A loud insistent knock wrested Denver from his cocoon of deep slumber. He ignored it. It came again through the pile of woolen blankets, penetrating his sleep.

"Mr. Johnson!" a woman's voice called. "Noreen here! Wake up! I'll wait in my car while you get dressed."

His mind ran through the condition of his home: the dust gathered on tabletops, spider webs on the drapes, empty tin cans that had held Campbell's tomato soup and Dinty Moore beef stew. Pills from Emma's last prescriptions were on a plastic Lazy Susan in the middle of the kitchen table, along with bottles of vitamins and aspirin. In a pile, coupons Emma had planned to use on her next trip to the grocery store.

He'd forgotten, or tried to ignore, Noreen's promise to come on Monday.

Slowly, he reached an arm out of the covers, pulling his body up into the chilly air. He would have to get the fire going. His clothes lay draped atop his cowboy boots in a stiff pile next to the bed. He put them on, stood, and roughly ran his hand through his hair.

Downstairs, he looked out the window and saw Noreen waiting in a tan 1947 Studebaker. He opened the door and nodded briefly.

"Mornin', Mr. Johnson."

Noreen entered, carrying a large brown purse and wearing an orange-striped housedress similar to one Emma had worn, tucked slightly at the waist, and an old brown sweater with threads pulling loose at the elbows.

"Mornin', Noreen."

She came in, looked around, and shivered a little. "You gonna stoke up that fire?"

"I was fixin' to." Denver tried to say something else, but she waved him toward the stove, set down her bag, and reached inside. Out of the corner of his eye, he saw her pull out a bandanna, fold it into a triangle, and tie it over her head. "I should've called you. I don't need…"

"Now, Mr. Johnson. Don't you be talkin' about not needing anyone. It's plain to see you're drownin' out here, trying to take care of yourself and the place."

"I'm all right," he growled, stuffing some newspapers and kindling inside the black potbelly stove. Turning a handle that opened the flu into the stovepipe, he shoved in two larger pieces of wood, struck a match, and watched the flames leap as he closed the door.

The stove sat almost exactly in the middle of the square two-story house, so the warmth eventually permeated the entire place. Additional warmth was supplied by a cook stove in the kitchen. Near it was the back door, where almost everyone entered the house. The life, energy, and sustenance of the place had been in the kitchen. With Emma's death, the tomato sauce, the apple crisps, the life source — all were gone.

Noreen glanced over her shoulder. Next to the kitchen, the dining area contained a large round oak table, obscured under piles of mail and old newspapers.

The living room, carpeted in beige, held a wide comfortable recliner where, she imagined, Denver usually sat, an avocado green couch, a matching mahogany wood-veneer coffee table and end tables, each holding a milk-glass lamp.

As Noreen worked in the kitchen, Denver noticed Emma's pills on the table and feared that Noreen might throw them out. Quickly, he grabbed as many as he could and shoved them in a drawer.

Noreen was rattling pans in the kitchen, aware of what he was doing, but silent.

"A fire in the cook stove would help take the frost off and I could fix some food. I brought some biscuits. Do you have any eggs?" Noreen asked, turning to the refrigerator, opening the door, bending over, and looking inside.

He walked toward her. "Emma might not like you in her kitchen."

"Emma or you? She'd want things taken care of. She wouldn't want you starving."

"Guess not," he mumbled.

Noreen stepped away from the kitchen, moving toward the tall upright piano against the far wall in the living room. On top of it was a family gathering of sorts—pictures of various relatives, most in cardboard frames.

"Your children?" she said, gesturing toward the pictures.

"Yup!" Denver said. He looked at the pictures first, without explaining, then slowly, he began. "That's Harold, our oldest son."

Harold was in military uniform. Noreen had heard the news when it filtered through town that this young man was deployed as part of the Eighth Armored Division, the day that stretch of the Normandy coast became known as Omaha Beach.

"He's buried over there. Under a white cross." Denver said, thinking of his son in an American cemetery in France.

Noreen stood quietly before asking, "That's Martha and Benjamin getting married isn't it?"

"Yes, and Elizabeth, 'course, with Daniel. William when he graduated college. He was the first one in our family to do that."

"It's a nice family, Denver. I'm sorry about Harold. He gave his life for his country. So many did. Still, you're blessed to have the others."

"Yes. Sometimes it seems like the ones who are gone are still here, like I almost expect to see them. They were here. This has been the family home for over fifty years."

"That's a long time. You have a lot of memories here, and it hasn't been long since . . .." Without finishing the sentence, Noreen turned back to the kitchen, saying, "Now, I better be lookin' into that breakfast."

"My whole life has been here. Never lived anywhere else."

"Really? Were your parents homesteaders?"

"Yes." He'd learned everything he knew about farming from his father and brothers, though his father was not a farmer at heart. He lacked the plodding persistence, the reading of wind and weather, the patience to plow and caress the soil until it became pliable and fertile. When his father needed money or thought he saw an advantage — a better investment — he sold some of the 160 acres the family had homesteaded, until in the 1930s they owned only 40 acres.

"There's lots of history here."

"Yes, there is. Are you gonna get this here kitchen stove goin'?"

Moving to the cook stove, he realized that it hadn't been used much since Emma's death. White enamel with a black surface, it had two front doors, one to add fuel below the two burners, and the oven door. Like everything here, it stirred memories. Sometimes Emma would remove one of the black rounds and put a pan directly on the fire. Other times, she threw a little water across the hot surface, watching the wet drops skitter and roll — her way of gauging the heat.

Emma kept coal in a nearby bucket, which could be used after the fire was going well to maintain oven temperature for the hours needed to bake a turkey or a roast. She fixed soups and stews, pancakes, eggs, fried potatoes with onions, thickly-sliced bacon, and the long green beans that grew in the garden staked on slender pieces of wood.

Through the summer months, Emma spent most of her time between the garden and the kitchen, keeping herself, Martha, and Elizabeth busy.

Before dinner, Emma would ask everyone, "How many ears of corn can you eat?" Then she'd say, "Martha, go pick the corn. Elizabeth, get that big pot of water to boiling. The two of you shuck it and bring it in, so's we can have it for supper." As she spoke, Emma put her right hand on her hip, straightening her back, wiping hair from her face with the back of her other arm. By evening, the constant leaning into the stove and stooping to pull weeds or pick a ripe cucumber from the garden made her back ache. Still, she liked nothing better than when the shelves in the fruit cellar were lined with Kerr and Mason jars in quart and pint sizes, colorful fruit and vegetables inside: bright red tomatoes and strawberry jam, deep purple plums, the peaches with so much fuzz on the outside that you itched after handling them, green beans, and multicolored relishes.

Denver remembered when they added the second floor, and a bathroom. The bathtub was put in later, soon after World War II began. Its installation received the same kind of appreciation a wood floor did after the dirt one his family had for years.

"Would you look at that?" Emma had stared at the newly delivered white glazed object. "Would you just look at that?"

"Can I take the first bath?" Elizabeth, their youngest daughter, asked.

"Well, child, it isn't hooked up yet. We'll see," Her mother replied.

"Why should she get to take the first one?" Martha, the elder daughter, wanted to know.

"Your mother will take the first one." Denver settled the matter.

"We will have to be very careful about cleaning it. You must wash it down when you get out. Now, let's get to work." Emma prompted them back to their duties.

While Denver ruminated, Noreen found the remnants of a ham. She sliced and fried it along with eggs, "over easy" as Denver ordered them in the café, and served it with the biscuits.

Denver ate quietly and with relish. It was the first food that had tasted good in a long time.

Noreen sat across from Denver, drinking coffee. She glanced at the remaining pills and coupons on the table.

"The medicines," Noreen said quietly, "Do you have any use for them?"

"Dunno. Don't do anything with them."

"Okay. I just thought…it might help…."

"You…you can't come into my house and tell me what to do! I knew it wouldn't work. I'll see you out." Anger flew in him.

"I'll leave if you like, but you could use some help. I won't touch the pills."

Her calm voice settled the storm within him. "Well, I s'pose it's all right. Least, we'll try it for a bit."

Perhaps realizing she had overstepped some invisible barrier, she sought to explain. "My mother told me I was a C-plus person." She brought her voice up slightly at the end of each sentence as if pressing the listener to respond, adding a tentative note to all her speech.

"What'd she mean by that?" he asked.

"Well, she wanted me to know that I was no prize, and that life wouldn't be easy for me. That whatever I got from it would be by pulling, tugging, and insisting upon it. I don't think she meant anything else. She just wanted me prepared." Noreen got up, walked to the stove, picked up the aluminum coffee pot that perked at the back, and brought it to fill their cups, doing it as automatically as she would at the café.

"Take your Emma," Noreen said, startling Denver by using his wife's name. "She was beautiful, and she had something about her, I think, don't you? A wise soul. She must have felt special — A-plus — must have known from the beginning that men were going to be throwing their jackets down for her to walk on. I used to watch her when she came to town, you know. She was a few years older than me."

"She never expected nothin' to be handed to her." Denver was uncomfortable with Noreen's talk about Emma. She was his private treasure. "She wasn't like that."

"But she could have been. She was quality. Ya' see my point?"

Denver nodded. Emma would see something disturbing in the assessment Noreen's mother had made of her daughter, or perhaps just that she had made it. It was something like giving out a grade before class had begun.

Not needing much encouragement to talk, Noreen continued. "I knew I had to study, to mind, and not get into trouble. I smiled at everyone, thinkin' they might like me."

"No reason not to."

"Emma had such pretty hair. My Momma always used to say to me, 'What are we going to do with that hair, girl?' Then she commenced to brush it hard, until my scalp hurt. She parted it in the middle and again into three sections on each side and braided it, pulling all the time. 'It hurts, Momma,' I said sometimes, but she went right on and said, 'I'll show you hurt,' and waved the hairbrush in front of my face. Sometimes I cried, but I sat still. Every Saturday night, after my bath, she did my hair."

"Hrump." Denver cleared his throat. He'd seen this Eckers girl most of his life, but never paid her much regard. Her parents had owned the general store and lived over it until it went out of business after the war, when Albertson's Grocery was built, with its big aisles, bright shiny cases, and neon lights that shone down on more packaged food than he'd known existed. He didn't know if her parents were alive, or if they still lived around here. He didn't ask.

Noreen looked around. "I should get on with cleanin' now, if you've had enough to eat. Will you show me where the cleaning stuff is?"

"Yes," he said, but didn't move from the table.

"You go ahead and sit a while longer. I'll do up these dishes." She rose from the table, giving him space to slip away again.

Denver used to think that Emma had come out of the earth, she was so much a part of it. Where he wrested a living from reluctant soil, for her, working the land was like growing babies, nurturing and watching each development, adapting, using, and taking pleasure in the slightest change. A new word. A new shoot.

"Emma's outside a lot in the summer," Denver mumbled to himself. He saw her standing in the garden, leaning over to check the radishes and lettuce. Emma never wanted to be anywhere else. It was as if she had drawn a circle around their home, and then a larger one around the community of Kuna. Those circles held her world. She rarely read the paper, as if, beyond what she could touch, taste, and smell, it was all a slippery fiction.

Digging in the dirt like a child at play, she exulted in the rich loam she helped create. She taught her daughters how to bury gladioli bulbs, coddle tiny squash, find tomato bugs, and water the rows of vegetables once they'd been cleaned of weeds and pests.

Martha and Elizabeth listened, but they were not of the soil. While their mother reveled in nature and its patterns, in taming, fondling, bending, and using the dirt to create sustenance for her family, her daughters impatiently bided their time.

They had been to town—or heard of it. All during the war years, Martha and Elizabeth bent their ears over the large Motorola console radio at the far end of the house from the kitchen.

That day when Denver brought the radio home in the back of the pickup, everyone except Emma was excited. Harold and William, working in a field near the house, dropped their hoes and ran over as their father got out. Ten-year-old Martha, with her dark hair and sharp features, came running from the garden. Never wanting to miss anything, eight-year-old Elizabeth, who looked like her mother, came out of the house, slamming the screen door. Both girls wore flowery print dresses sewn by their mother from feed sacks that had been filled with mash or grain brought home from the feed store.

The large cardboard carton was tied onto the back of the truck. Denver and the boys tore the knots from the rope that held it.

"Where's your mother?" Denver asked the children.

"She's in the kitchen. Mom!" Elizabeth called. Emma came to the door with a kitchen towel in her hand, but advanced no further. While the children clamored excitedly, a part of Denver knew that Emma's brow furrowed underneath the rich hair. He wanted to go to her and smooth the ridges.

"We've no place for that, Denver," Emma said and went back into the house.

Harold and William, in the back of the pickup, tugged and pulled at the big box.

"Push it along easy now," their father instructed. "We'll have to get some boards to slide it off the back."

When this was accomplished and they had the radio almost to the house, Emma opened the door and said, "I don't know where you're gonna put that." Then, finally, "Keep it far from my kitchen. I won't have you sitting around idly listening!"

Slowly, the radio came into the house — a presence she did not want to acknowledge. As the rest of the family crowded around it, running an extension cord, moving a bookshelf, Emma banged pots and mumbled to herself about "any work getting done today."

New voices came through the house. Winter evenings, all four children crowded round and listened

to The Green Hornet, Fibber McGee and Molly, and
Stella Dallas. Denver sat nearby.

"Come on, Emma. Come sit down," he would call
to her. If she did, she sat a little stiffly and brought a
sock to darn, or a hem to stitch. Emma never just sat
except in church. Always, there was work to be done.

"My fellow Americans! I hate war! Eleanor hates
war!" The Johnsons had listened to the warm tones of
President Franklin Delano Roosevelt and were drawn
into a larger circle of concern.

Like the radio, the war wormed itself into their
lives as something that could not be disregarded.
They listened as Walter Winchell, Edward R. Mur-
row, and President Roosevelt spoke, giving the con-
flict a tangible cause, like weather that must be prepared for, a pest to be eradicated, or a fire requiring
containment.

"I have a pain in my stomach when I hear all this
talk of war," Emma told Denver. In front of them, the
shoulders of their eldest son, Harold, grew rigid. His
intense blue eyes stared at the radio, his hair falling
forward as he leaned to hear more clearly. His fair
skin and medium build — he was 5'8" — came from his
English heritage. His wrists were slim and too small
to hold a rifle. Thank goodness, he was too young.

That did not save him, though. The day he hopped
into the pickup with his dad, went into the recruiter's
office, and lied about his age, Denver was scared, but
respectful too, of his son going to war. Emma was
struck dumb when they returned and told her. She
stared at them as if something foreign had replaced

the two she knew. Somewhere in the flat Idaho farmland, the child she bore and the man she loved had
been replaced by this young man who was excited
about going to war and his stunned, but proud, father.

"You go back down there, Denver. You tell them
he is not old enough. You take his birth certificate."
Emma pushed the document toward her husband.

He shook his head. "They know how old he is. It
was Fred Barnes in the office there. He has a son the
same age—Jeff. He's going with Harold."

"You went with him?"

"No. I was across at the feed store. He came and
told me, so then I went over and talked to Barnes. It's
our country, Emma," Denver said.

"It's that radio. Those voices make war exciting.
He's fifteen, for goodness sake!" She sat on the edge
of the bed.

"But he wants to go. He wants to fight for his
country."

"Where will he go? The Pacific Islands? North Af-
rica? Doesn't matter. They're just spots of color on a
map. Every day, boys Harold's age die there. No one
knows who they are," Emma said.

"The army does. The army takes care of our boys.
Two of my brothers served in the First World War.
They came home all right," he replied.

"They came home." Her response came slow and
heavy. "One of 'em said to me, who it was, I'm not
sure, said he'd been to hell and back. Yes, it was Ches-

ter. I asked him what he meant. He stared at me, really beyond me. I read something terrible in his eyes. Pain, fear, I don't know what all. 'Nothin' for a lady to hear.' When he said that, his voice was cold and desperate. I asked him, I said, 'If you was to tell it, who could you say it to?' He looked at me again and his eyes glistened as he said, 'You're the first one who ever really wanted to know. I started talkin' 'bout it a few times when I first came home. Folks turned away, or said it's over now — best put it behind us. I was so filled with the war when I came home, Emma, I was ready to explode. I could still feel my friend's head as he lay dying, right here.' He reached out with the stub of his left arm and touched the flesh of his right one where it bent. 'Right here, Emma. It wasn't quick and neat like bein' alive one moment and dead the next. It was real slow and…the pain was awful. His face half gone. His body broken like a clod of dirt that had been thrown.' Chester looked at me and he said, 'Now you don't wanna hear no more, do you?' Though I did not turn away or stop him, I shivered. We both were quiet. I was relieved when someone called us to dinner, though I couldn't eat."

"You're gonna do yourself no good by thinkin' 'bout that now," Denver told her.

"What else would you have me think about?"

That night in bed, they both stared at the ceiling. Denver — and he was certain Emma too — saw strange and foreign lands, distant fields, not unlike his land, where crops were grown. Now, nothing grew. Men fought. Many of those young men would never experience the freedom they fought for. Surely, America and its allies would win. America never lost.

As much as anything, Denver realized, the boy was looking for excitement. Perhaps he had looked at his father—the endless days, the backbreaking labor—and saw himself in twenty or forty years shoveling manure and dirt, worrying about weather and pinching pennies, holding on precariously to a life pulled reluctantly from the soil.

Harold, like his father and grandfather, was not of the soil as Emma was. He did not love it. Each of them had needed it and hated their dependence on it. Maybe Harold would not have to be a farmer. He went to school through the entire session, not just in winter, as Denver had.

What had the boy thought, lying in the next room before going to war?

In the three days before he left, Harold looked past his mother and father without seeing them, as if his life had been absorbed into some larger cause. Before Emma could finish knitting him woolen stockings, he was gone.

They drove him to the train station in Nampa, the children sitting in the back of their Model-T Ford. All of them wore their Sunday best. On the platform, dozens of families said good-bye. There was cheering.

Denver stepped forward to speak to someone. Turning back toward Emma, he saw her normally ruddy countenance turned ashen and knew her terror. Her hands shook. The girls and young William, flushed with color and the excitement of the crowd, stepped forward. Emma backed away.

Denver saw that she faded from the inside out. In some vague part of his mind, he saw other mothers—quiet, stick figures at the rear of the crowd—who could not join the day's celebration, who had watched, protected, and shielded these children from conception to this day and couldn't take care of them any longer.

He read agony on the faces of Emma and the other mothers and thought they were screaming inside in a protest so primal it began at the base where the drive to create and continue life begins. Their minds knew the facts. Their ears heard the excited crowd, the patriotic feeling, but it was all just noise.

"War brings death," Emma told Denver that day. "I can't celebrate sending Harold to kill others, or be killed."

On the drive home, Emma sat woodenly looking out the window. "I don't know what I'm supposed to do now, or why."

"Send him things, Momma! The socks you're knitting and gloves," Elizabeth said.

"I'm going to bake him something—a cake, Momma," Martha said. "Help me, Momma. Tell me what recipe will make cake that lasts long enough so it will be good when he gets it." She leaned forward and placed her hand on the pink cotton fabric on her mother's shoulder.

"Can I sleep in Harold's bed?" William asked. The two boys slept in bunk beds. Both had wanted the top space. As the older boy, Harold had slept there.

"Well, that would probably be all right. Do you think so, dear?" Denver had asked his wife.

"I don't see any reason why not. Never understood why you both wanted to sleep on top. Used to worry about Harold falling out. It's hotter up there in the summer."

"It's a little bit like floating, Momma. You close your eyes, and you're off the ground—flying," William replied.

Each of the children, that day, pulled their mother back, knowing of her wound and wanting to heal her.

William held her hand when they got out of the car at home. I'm your son, Momma. Love me. I will stay with you, he seemed to be saying.

Emma heard and responded. They settled back into their rural life. Everyone wrote to Harold, though letters from Denver were rare. The children raced each other to the mailbox each day to see if a letter had arrived. Emma, too, stopped what she was doing and joined the others crowding around the radio for the war reports.

Noreen was looking at Denver.

He had not touched the mop or broom since Emma died. Once Martha had come over to clean, but he was gruff with her. "Don't move my papers, or none of your mother's stuff," he told her repeatedly, and then sat in his recliner glaring at her.

"Why don't you go out and leave the house to me?" Martha asked.

"I don't know what you'll do with it. Won't be able to find things. I told you I'd take care of it," Denver replied.

"I'm not stayin' where I'm not wanted." Martha put on her jacket in a huff and left without saying good-bye.

Denver knew that Emma wouldn't want things to get ragged between him and the children, but he didn't know how to iron out the differences and smooth the corners. He'd never been entirely easy with his oldest daughter.

She'd begun dating Benjamin while in high school. When he drove down the lane to their house the first time, he honked the horn.

"You just wait here, young woman." Emma had required this, and Martha fumed as she peeked out the window. "He knows better than that."

"Yes, he does, but he's a football player. Thinks he can get away with anything," Denver said.

"He's not like that." Martha looked in the mirror, adjusting her blouse.

"You make sure he's not," her mother said.

He had come to the door then. The size of his body, the large muscles across his shoulders and back, the meaty thighs and forearms, dominated the room as he entered. His black, thick and wavy hair was shiny from the greasy hair tonic holding it in place. Small dark eyes peered out at the family from a fleshy cave.

Martha had made an uncertain move toward him.

Reluctantly, Denver stood, took a step toward the hulking figure, and put out his hand. "Denver Johnson."

"Benjamin Samuels." Taking Denver's hand, he squeezed hard.

Denver flinched slightly. "This is Martha's mother, Emma Johnson."

"How's your family, then? Do come and sit down." Emma gestured toward the sofa.

"Momma," Martha said, softly protesting. She was standing next to Benjamin.

Emma had ignored her daughter and gestured toward the couch. The large youth took a step, turned, and sat down, swiping a small figurine off the coffee table as he did. Martha bent to pick it up. A small piece had broken off and she felt along the floor until she found it, then put it back in place, testing whether it could be fixed.

Emma disregarded the broken figurine. "How's your mother? I heard she was sick awhile back."

Elizabeth and William came in and were introduced. Denver noticed that Benjamin's eyes rested on Elizabeth for some time. Everyone sat forward in their chairs, tense and ill at ease.

Benjamin cleared his throat. "She's doing better now."

"Oh, good. Tell her I asked after her." Emma said.

A nervous silence had filled the room.

"Well, I guess we should be going." Benjamin looked at Martha. "The movie starts pretty soon."

She had a light pink sweater in her hand and wore a deeper pink blouse and flared dark blue skirt. She'd spent most of the day curling her hair and deciding what to wear.

The young man stood up slowly, testing whether he would be commanded to sit down again.

"Martha, you know the rules," Emma said.

"Yes, Momma."

"Have a good time, then. Nice to meet you, Benjamin. Give my best to your family."

"Nice to meet you." Denver's left hand gestured toward the door. Benjamin noticed the missing finger and looked again at the older man. "How…?" Then dropping the question, he followed Martha out the door.

Denver stayed up that evening until his daughter came home.

"Were you waiting up for me?" Martha's hands moved quickly to smooth her clothes.

"No. No. Did you have a good time?"

"Yes."

"Good." He pulled himself forward in the chair. "Well, it's time to get to bed." He stood as Martha started down the hall. "You be careful, you hear. You take care of yourself. I can't…." He stopped, feeling the old helplessness, the world spinning away from him and his inability to stop it.

"Can't what, Poppa?"

"I can't protect you from yourself. We try. We'll always try."

"I know, Poppa. I'm not Elizabeth. She'll have lots of guys chasing her. I don't."

"Now don't fret about that. One good one—that's all you need, and there's no hurry."

"One. Good night, Poppa."

Martha married Benjamin in 1948. A year later, Bobbie was born, then Benjamin, and lastly, Sally, in 1952.

Chapter Three

As he watched Noreen glance around the house, Denver knew that Emma would be mortified that anyone — Noreen Eckers even — would see their home in this condition.

"Make your bed as soon as you get out of it," Emma told the children. They never left for school until their beds were smooth and their rooms in order.

Now, Noreen banged dishes in the kitchen. "Soon as I get these dishes done, I'll commence with the cleaning. What are you going to do today?"

She worked, he thought, with more gusto and less efficiency than Emma — spilling some dishwater on the floor, not taking quite as much care with the scrubbing. Still, she was there, bringing with her some inkling of forward movement.

As she dried the skillets and hung them from hooks on the wall, put dishes away in the cupboard, dishrag and towels on a dowel near the stove to dry, she talked — whether Denver was listening or not.

It was her way of connecting and holding on in the world, Denver thought. He couldn't do it. With him, events, words, his life, were bundled tightly inside, unexposed. Now, it all seemed to be unwinding, playing again.

"I was tellin' you about my Momma," Noreen said. "She had me wear the clothes that didn't sell in the store. Still new, of course, just rack weary. I remember an orange and green dress. After it hung at the back of the store through two or three seasons, looked at and rejected by everybody in town, Momma gave it to me for my birthday. 'Thank you, Momma,' I said, trying to hide my disappointment. I didn't want to wear it. No sir. Not the dress that no one else wanted. Momma just said, 'We'll pin it here and here.' Not alter it, mind you. 'It will work fine. Lots of girls never have a new dress. Most of 'em wear dresses made from those feed sacks! Hand-me-downs.' She stopped for a minute, then added, 'Just look at that cake!'"

Denver saw Noreen glance in his direction to see if he was listening, if she was keeping him, briefly, from the past, where he so often slipped.

"Momma lit ten candles on the yellow birthday cake. We bought things from the bakery across the street, so each year Aunt Hilda — that's what I called the lady at the bakeshop — baked a birthday cake and gave it to me. Momma invited her up to celebrate with us.

"I remember one time — I'd forgotten all about this, but Hilda was always nice to me — she heard my momma call me her C-plus daughter. She said to me, when we were alone, 'You're better than that, Noreen, better than C-plus.' I'd forgotten that."

"Seems like you might want to remember it," Denver said.

Noreen turned and looked at him full face, as if his words had lit a dark place in her. "You're right about that. Momma never wanted me to get too big for my britches. She didn't set the ladder too high for me."

"Don't take your meaning, exactly. Better be gettin' on, I suppose." He spoke in a gruff tone and rose from the table as if to ward off any intimacy she might infer from the conversation.

"Now, before you go out — how 'bout that cleanin' stuff? Reckon I could find it myself."

He moved awkwardly through the kitchen, as if finding his way through unfamiliar ground. She expected him to go outside and work.

He had no plan for the land that was his simply because he continued to exist on it. When his parents died, his seven brothers and two sisters agreed that Denver, since he was the one who lived there, should have it as long as he worked it. If he wanted to sell it, they would have to talk about it again. That was over twenty years ago. Most of them had gone to California in the late '20s or early '30s when falling food prices and the smoldering infection that became the Depression thrust itself upon the country.

Noreen, elbows akimbo, watched him and waited.

"I think you'll find the cleaning stuff under the sink. And, let's see," he opened the back door onto the porch. "Here's a mop and broom," he said. "The Hoover's in the hall closet."

"Fine. I'll take it from there. Now, you best get out from underfoot and let me clean."

He closed the door and walked heavily back through the house as if it wasn't his, as if this strange woman had advanced upon it with intent to change it in some indefinable way. "Don't be openin' drawers. If you clean the surfaces, that'll be plenty."

"Ah-h. It certainly will."

He retreated upstairs to the bedroom and bath, eating up time as if it were a meal he didn't relish. Finally, he put on his jacket and came down.

Noreen had begun dusting. "These newspapers. Should I throw them out?"

"I—I been aimin' to read them."

"Aimin's one thing. Firing's another."

He felt a slight grin edging along the corner of his mouth, but looked away so she wouldn't see it. "Well, throw out most of 'em. Save last week's."

"What about all this mail? Should I put it in a pile on the table so you can go through it?"

"That'd be fine."

"Unless you want to go through it now."

"No. No. I've got work to do outside."

"I'll scare up somethin' for lunch 'bout noon. If you can spare the time."

"Yes, ma'am." He opened the back door, stepping onto the porch. He would have to appear busy, though he didn't wish to think ahead. Planting, irrigating morning to night through the hot Idaho summer, and harvesting whatever crop it might be — all implied effort he couldn't comprehend in his inert state. He hadn't contracted, as most farmers did, with Simplots, Crookhams, or the Idaho Sugar Beet Company. His nose prickled with the remembered stink from the sugar beet factory. Perhaps he could still make an agreement.

He'd planted fewer acres in row crops in the last couple of years. Two five-acre fields lay fallow. He rented some land out as pasture, but the rent did little more than pay the water bill.

"You aren't doing much farmin' these days," a neighbor had said to Denver when Emma lay ill. "Seems like you need to, her bein' sick and all. Doctors don't come cheap."

"Well, course, she's got to be cared for," Denver had muttered.

"Martha and Elizabeth come over and take care of things," Emma had said. "They take turns cooking meals. They do the wash and hang it on the line."

"I bring it in sometimes," Denver mumbled, defensively.

"Yes, but they clean the house. They take care of me most of the time. You're confused — stumbling around like you have two left feet. Fretting over what is going to happen next." Emma's reply was sensible, as she always was.

"I . . . I can't see life beyond you."

"Denver Johnson, you listen to me. We've had twenty-eight good years. You know how to farm. You keep right on a doin' it."

"Why? I did it for you. To be with you is all I ever wanted from the first time I saw you."

"There's the children, Denver. And the good memories—the grandkids. Oh, how I wish I could see them grow up. Do you know how lucky you are, Denver? You will be alive! Damn you!" She'd never sworn before. "You go on smelling the earth, do it for me, and that rose bush you gave me that has the red blossoms. I planted that under our bedroom window. Taste a ripe tomato, and a plum. Feel. Touch. Taste. Denver, do it for me. Because I can't."

"I hadn't thought of it that way."

This spring morning, with Noreen in the house, he walked toward the barn. The tractor had been stored inside through the winter. He wondered if it would start. Lifting the wooden latch that held the big double doors closed, he slowly pulled one side open. It scraped against the ground. He stopped a couple of times to kick away tumbleweeds and a rock that were in the way.

The darkness inside was interrupted here and there where a shingle had torn from the roof or a wallboard had warped and bent so a shaft of light pierced the black. Straw covered the ground.

The air was musty and carried a latent smell of cow dung, hay, and yesterday. An old, old jacket that had been his father's hung from a ten-penny nail on the wall. He couldn't touch it, afraid, somehow, that his father still lived inside it.

He moved through the darkness toward a window held shut by a hook and opened it, the metal hinges creaking from lack of use. By the time he opened a half-dozen windows, the day filtered in, illuminating the shape of plows, the row of shovels and pitchforks on the wall, and the line of stanchions built to hold the cows' heads in place.

"Denver," he heard Noreen's voice calling, and felt it an intrusion.

She reached the open barn door and stopped. "Will it run?" She pointed at the tractor.

"I don't know. Just been checking it out."

"Martha called. She's coming over with the children."

"Why?"

"Well, the phone rang. I figured I should answer it. Hope that's okay." She paused until he nodded. "She wanted to know who I was and what I was doing here. She didn't ask 'bout comin' over. She told me. So, I said you would be in soon for lunch."

"Well, can you manage it—lunch for everyone, I mean?"

"Yes. It'll be soup and bread, but I reckon that'll do."

"Yes. That will be fine. Set a place for yourself." He turned back to the tractor, swiping his hand across the words "John Deere." Now there was a man who was successful—his name rumbling across farmland all across the country and in every farm town from here to Pennsylvania.

"I wonder. Could you come in a little early and do something with that pile of mail? I hate to move it," Noreen asked.

"Yes. I'll be in shortly." Denver, so far, was unable to get a grip and move forward with planning crops for the year. Sorting the mail might be easier. Martha would come, demanding to know what, and why, and wherefore, wanting something from him that he'd misplaced or couldn't identify.

As Noreen walked back to the house, Denver climbed on the tractor. It started easily. He edged it out of the barn and into the sunlight. Maybe he would see about raising sugar beets.

"Denver, you work this farm," Emma admonished him as she lay dying. "You make me proud. You've never been completely on your own. Now you will be. You're a good man, Denver Johnson—diligent, quiet, respectful, but you'll have to change some after I die." Denver thought she noted mentally his limitations, though she was too kind to say them aloud. "You best marry again, dear. You'll need someone to help you."

Inside, he was reading the mail, wearing drug-store bifocals, when he heard car doors slamming and the high-pitched voices of the children. Seconds later, they burst into the house.

"Granddad!"

Six-year-old Bobbie, with his dark, curly hair bouncing and an eager glint in his eye, led the charge, followed by his brother, Benjy, who was five, with lighter brown hair and a sturdy body, and three-year-old Sally, the lightest and fairest of the three, a troop ready to do whatever their older brother said. Their mother, like a distant general, hadn't entered yet.

The boys didn't approach their grandfather, but Sally came over, stood next to him, and pulled at his coat, so he leaned over. She kissed him on the cheek.

Out the window, Denver saw his daughter looking around—first toward the barn, then at the slender, emerging daffodil tips.

Elizabeth, his younger daughter, looked like Emma. Martha had fine brown hair which never held its shape, a wide face, and large ears, like her father. Smart in school, Martha picked up everything quickly—spelling, arithmetic, and her mother's directions on domestic duties.

"This fall, now, these bulbs will have to be dug up," Martha said without preamble as she came in through the back door. She glanced toward her children, who'd found the toy box. She turned to Noreen. "I'm Martha Samuels. You work at the café?"

"Yes."

"Do you clean for folks on the side? I know they can't pay much at Lily's."

Denver could see Noreen flush with embarrassment at his daughter's assessment of her.

"Well, not regularly. I offered to help your dad out." Noreen turned toward the stove.

"Whatever happened to . . . what was his name—your husband?" Martha asked.

"Don. He's not my husband, hasn't been for five years." Noreen responded.

"Oh."

"Hello, Martha," Denver interjected.

"Why do you let her clean the house when you won't let me?"

"Well, I thought you had your hands full, with these young 'uns and your own house and husband. I guess I wasn't ready before."

"I wouldn't have offered if I was neglecting anything. I'm your daughter. I'm not just anybody. A stranger. You wouldn't let me touch anything." She grumbled

"Benjamin busy with plowin', is he? I'm thinkin' of getting out there myself after lunch."

"Can I ride on the tractor with you, Granddad?" Bobbie asked.

"Me, too," Benjy and Sally chimed in.

"We're leaving after lunch, children. Now, come and sit down at the table."

Noreen ladled vegetable soup into each bowl and sat down quietly, clearly undone in the presence of Martha.

"Bobbie, will you say the blessing?" his mother asked.

The boy leaned forward slightly. Putting his small palms together and placing them in front of him, he began, "Lord we thank you for this food." Though Bobbie didn't resemble Harold, Denver was reminded of his oldest son. Fair-haired Harold would always be fifteen. That death was when Emma had ceased wanting to live, though it had taken over a decade to completely extinguish her vitality.

Rumors of a large invasion from Great Britain across the English Channel had come to the family from the radio. Planes overhead, ships in the water, and troops everywhere, the attack would take the Nazis by surprise—though how could that be with these stories on the air? Harold had written; the letter was posted in London.

"I've seen Buckingham Palace. The Tower of London. It's another world, really. I drink beer. It's different over here. We practice hard and wait. I'm excited and a little scared."

Emma sat by the radio day and night, once they received reports that the invasion was on, as if that hated radio might say, "Harold Johnson is alive in France." She shuddered with the reports of high casualties and listened for the company names and numbers.

With reports of heavy losses, Emma sank into despondency.

"Look. Our peach tree is going to give us a bumper crop this year." Denver had tried to bring her back.

She looked at him as if he had lost his mind. "Don't talk to me of peaches. My son is dead. I know it, Denver."

"You don't know that."

"Yes, I do. The telegram will come tomorrow . . . or soon." Her voice was flat.

The wire came. When Emma saw the message, she slumped to the floor, wretchedly sobbing, and pounding the wood until she exhausted herself. They couldn't do anything with her. For months, she walked inconsolably through the house, scarcely seeing the tasks that, before, she had taken up with enthusiasm. Peaches rotted. Tomatoes went unplanted. Life took a hiatus, so great was the war's destruction upon her.

The reports of casualties on the battlefield kept coming. Later they learned of the extermination camps in Germany. The living grappled with the deaths—excusing, denying, asking forgiveness, recounting, and asking why—while trying to reconstruct a new life from the ruins.

Emma's all-consuming grief and continued distraction had been hard for the other children. She had guided and nurtured them before, but now it was as if she too was a casualty of the war.

Martha had been fourteen at the time. She'd filled in for her mother—running the household and guiding her younger siblings. Later, she and Elizabeth took care of domestic chores and their mother when she lay dying.

Pulling himself back to the present, Denver turned to face his daughter. "Martha. I don't know that I ever told you, but when your brother died in the war and your mother sort of fell apart, you filled in. When your mother was dying, you took care of her. You've been a good daughter."

The children grew still and looked at their mother.

A glistening in her eyes was the only immediate response. Denver saw that his words opened something in her, some secret closet long ignored. She cleared her throat. "I reckon if you want to take the children for a ride on the tractor, maybe I could give Noreen a hand here in the house for a while."

"What do you say to that, boys?" Denver asked.

"Me too, Granddad," Sally said.

"You'll have to take turns. Can Martha give you a hand, Noreen?" Denver asked.

"There's plenty to do," Noreen said.

"You gonna get your cow back, Granddad?" Bobbie asked. Denver's one remaining cow, Lady, was still in the pasture at Martha's home.

"Well, I suppose I could one of these days. Martha, you might ask Benjamin 'bout that. He borrowed the cattle trailer when he took her."

"I'll talk to him, Pa. And, thank you for what you said." Martha remarked. "There's so much history in this house. So much death."

"You're right about that. I rattle around here . . . it comes back to me. All that happened here. My parents never said anything; they just expected me to take care of them and run the farm. That directed my whole life."

"And I was about Sally's age when my grandparents died here." Martha shuddered. "Course, they do it differently now, but then, the body stayed right in the house until the funeral. Folks came. I remember Harold and me sneakin' up to the coffin and peekin' in to see if Grandma had changed. We heard that fingernails kept growin' and we wanted to see if they had."

"Did they?" Bobbie asked.

"I don't think so. I don't remember. All I recall… she was…like a stranger." Martha replied.

"What do you mean, Momma?" Benjy asked.

"I can't explain it, except that people say the dead look like they're sleepin'. That's true, except there's a difference."

"The spirit has left the body and gone back to God," Noreen said.

"I guess that's it. It just didn't seem like that body was Grandma. It was, and it wasn't."

"Seems to me, if you'll pardon my saying so," Noreen said, "so much living has gone on here. That's what makes the dying matter."

"I like how you put that," said Martha.

"Momma told me that my Uncle Harold died in the war." Bobbie's voice grew excited.

"He was 'fenden his country. My daddy told me so," Benjy said.

"When I grow up," Bobbie began, half-sliding out of his chair and standing beside it as if to appear bigger, "I'm gonna be a soldier."

"Me, too." Benjy put his hands together, pretending to hold a gun. "I'm gonna shoot Japs."

"No," Martha and her father said in unison.

"War isn't like a game of chase in the back yard. It's horrible," said Noreen.

"How do you know?" Bobbie asked.

"Did you go to war?" Benjy asked.

"No, silly. Girls don't go to war — well, some do, but men do the fighting," their mother answered.

"We all saw the pictures," Noreen said. "We heard the stories of people who were there. We said good-bye to boys just ten years older than you who never came back. I helped my folks in the general store during the war. I heard folks talk. You know, Bobbie and Benjy, when I wasn't much older than you, it was my job to see that the glass jars of penny candy were clean and shiny, so folks would buy some."

"I like candy," said Sally.

Noreen smiled at the little girl. "We had orange slices, red and black licorice, Boston Baked Beans, jelly beans, and striped hard candy. Folks would come in for flour, sugar, and salt. We wanted them to spend one more penny than they had planned."

Denver listened to her talk. Emma had spoken for him. Now, Noreen, with her direct ways, loosened something in him. It seemed natural, her being there.

At the end of that first day, he paid her from the meager amount in his checking account.

"Ya don't have to pay me. I offered to help."

"And you have, but that wouldn't be right. You done a good job. How much? I don't know what other folks pay for cleaning."

"I get fifty cents an hour at Lily's. And tips. And I eat breakfast and lunch there free. How about five dollars a day? Sound fair?"

"Yes, fair for me, but let's make it six." He wrote the check, tore it out of the book, and handed it to her. "You'll be back next Monday?"

"Yes. All right." She gathered her things and walked toward the door. "And I figure you'll have those fields plowed by then."

"If I'm gonna have help, I better make some money."

She looked back, one hand on the doorknob, uncertain perhaps about taking the money. Then, as if she had straightened it out in her mind, she said, "That's right, Mr. Johnson. You have obligations. You best be workin' to pay for them."

She left.

He felt adrift in the empty room.

Money from Emma's life insurance policy earned one percent in a savings account. He had three thousand dollars. That was all. By the time that was gone, he would have to be making money from the land or sell it, which he knew right out was a bad idea.

Where would he go if he didn't farm? He could probably do seasonal work at the sugar beet factory or at Pacific Fruit Express (PFE, they all called it), but he knew men were laid off there, too, from time to time. Neither place kept many men on through the winter.

He might not have farming in his blood, but he'd done it and been around it all his life. He knew how to do it, and the land was free and clear. As long as he could pay the taxes and the water bill, no one would take it away from him. His brothers and sisters would have something to say if he sold it.

Chapter Four

In the next few days, Denver contracted to sell ten acres of beets and began preparing the field. The land required plowing, removing rocks, and adding fertilizer. He got off the tractor frequently to move boulders. A wind from the west swirled plumes of dirt as it softened. It eventually crept inside his clothes and into his sparse hair until he was gritty.

The water in the shower at night ran brown.

Occasionally, when he climbed back on the tractor, he rested for a moment, looking across the Boise Valley, rimmed on the west by the Owyhee Mountains and the Boise Mountains to the east. Nearer, he saw a line of trees and another house and farm. Neighbors plowed their fields, sending little puffs of dirt into the air. Except for one trip to Los Angeles, he had never been anywhere beyond Boise, and there rarely.

It was possible to live in the same place all of your life and never see it. He seemed to be seeing it now through Emma's eyes and was glad for the sight.

The telephone rang one evening. Two long rings, the signal that the call was for Denver. He got few calls, though the phone rang frequently: eight families shared the line. A short ring — that would be for his neighbors, the Smiths. There were two shorts, as well as a long and short on his side of the party line. Four other families had rings on the other side of the line that he didn't hear.

He picked it up. "Hullo?"

"Hello, Denver. It's Benjamin. I can get that trailer tomorrow, so I thought I would bring Lady over. Okay?"

"Yes. I better check the fence to make sure she can't get out."

"That's a good idea."

"What time you figurin' on comin'?"

"Well, I suppose it'll be midday by the time I get there. That all right?"

"Yes. That'll be fine."

"That line's always busy," Elizabeth had complained when she was a teenager. Now she lived in town with her husband, Daniel, and had a private line. He worked at the bank and, according to some folks, was uppity.

He'd spent two years at Boise Junior College, more education than anyone else in the family. Daniel Robertson was a tall, good-looking man whose family lived in Boise and, as far as Denver knew, had never been farmers. That was a wide difference right there—living with the noise and currents of city people and being separated from the land and the open space of the country.

Emma and Denver had visited Daniel's parents in Boise, before the young folks married in June of 1950. His impression was that the Robertsons saw the two of them as slightly quaint and somehow charming.

Daniel Robertson was working at the bank in Kuna when he met Elizabeth. She won a school essay contest on "Why I'm Proud to Be an American." He represented the bank, presenting her with a twenty-five-dollar United States Savings Bond.

Daniel came to their home to court Elizabeth. He was polite and well-bred. Emma approved of the match. "Elizabeth wasn't made for the farm. She'll grow a few flowers around her house and be a lady."

"You're a lady," Denver said.

"Yes, but her fingernails will be clean and her hands soft. She'll have people in for dinner parties. She and Daniel will travel—not because someone has died, or even to see relatives. To see the world."

"Would you like to be that kind of a lady?"

"This is our life. I have no cause to complain. I love the world that I know—down to its smallest parts. The soil and how to work it. The winter sun glistening on the snow. That far line of trees bent in the wind. How the corn grows so fast in summer's heat. How you can see so far and you know what's yours. But I'm glad for Elizabeth. Still, she'll have her challenges."

Mr. Robertson had said, "We're proud to have our Daniel marrying into a solid farm family." The six of them had been sitting together in the dining room at the Robertson home with its large, dark, and shiny furniture, and the table set with fine china. "Farming is the backbone of this country."

"Yes," Emma had said. "Folks always need to eat."

"Right. Absolutely, and as more move off the farm, more need to buy food," said Mr. Robertson.

"Elizabeth brought some of your strawberry preserves one time when she came. They were wonderful. I admire your talents," Mrs. Robertson had said to Emma.

"It's not talent as much as practice," Emma responded. "I'd be glad to show you."

"Now, don't be modest, Mrs. Johnson," Daniel had said.

"Oh, yes. You'll have to show me some time," Mrs. Robertson had said. "More coffee anyone?"

After they married, Daniel and Elizabeth moved into a new house in Kuna. Daniel walked the few blocks to work at the bank. Sometimes, when they were in town for business, Denver and Emma would stop in to see their daughter in her new home.

"How are you feeling, dear?" Emma asked on one such occasion, when her daughter was pregnant.

"Fine. The doctor says everything's fine. I'm sewing these curtains for the baby's room. Come see." She led her mother into the bedroom.

The house smelled of fresh paint. Light seemed to fill every room. Outside, roses bloomed in a row between the grass and the sidewalk.

By this time, however, Emma was sick with something that would not go away. The brightness and life at Elizabeth's house made Denver ache.

"It's lovely, my dear," Denver heard Emma say. "You have a way with things, Lizzie. You make everything so pretty and pleasant."

"How are you feeling, Momma?"

"Well, the doc says I should take it easy. Don't like to, but I don't have much energy lately."

"But what is it, Momma? What really is wrong?"

"Well, it's a growth. I go back to the doctor next week."

"Where is it, Momma?"

"Here." Emma took Elizabeth's hand, as she had Denver's the night before, putting it on her lower abdomen and insisting that he feel the hard little knot there. It was the first time he had not taken pleasure in touching her.

"Will they take it out?"

He thought of the two women, each with a growth in the belly.

"Yes, I think so. It'll be all right, child. And I'm so happy for you. You've such a life to look forward to, such happy times. Daniel's a good man."

"If it's a boy, Momma, we want to name him Harold."

"That would be wonderful, dear."

"We'll get through this, Momma. I'll be with you, and you'll be with me."

Driving home that day, Emma said, "I'm so happy to see my children settled. My girls at least. And I think William will be all right."

"He's in school, Emma, college. Can you imagine? Me without enough education to be anything but a farmer."

"Don't say it doesn't take anything to be a farmer."

"That's not my meaning. William can work with his brain and his muscles. I never had enough book learnin' to have that choice."

"Well, I'm glad he's getting those two years in Boise, at least. He'll be like Daniel. He'll wear a suit and tie and go to work at an office." Denver thought she needed to secure the future for her children—in her mind, at least. "Looks like Martha will be the only one on a farm."

"Maybe William will come back to farmin'. This place has been in the family so long," Denver said.

Soon after, Elizabeth and Daniel, Martha and Benjamin, and William were with Denver, not knowing what to do or how to be in that strange land of the hospital. They were aliens, swallowed up in a foreign environment. Figures in white marched around giving orders, opening and closing doors with authority, or standing huddled together at something called the nurses' station, speaking an unfamiliar language.

The air smelled unnatural, chemical. Times and places were designated for visits from patients' families. They were subordinate to the mechanics of the system. The muted white, gray, and beige tones in walls, floors, and furnishings, along with the shiny chrome trays, added no life or punch to the atmosphere bereft of any of the familiar elements of sky, earth, and weather that dominated Denver and Emma's world.

Denver was lost, almost incoherent with fear and apprehension. He shoved it away into a back pocket when he was in Emma's room, but she could see it bulging there, affecting his every movement.

Elizabeth and Martha cut yellow and lavender gladiolas and bright pink peonies and brought them to their mother's room. William held his mother's hand, unsure of what to do or how to be.

Three months later, Elizabeth was in the hospital.

"You don't have to go there," Denver told Emma.

"I have to, but you don't. It's better where the babies are. People are happy."

"I suppose."

"Don't you see, I need to be with Elizabeth, to be there for the birth and to see the baby. I wouldn't miss that for the world."

"It's just, do you want to be at the hospital? Not the happiest place you've been."

"You haven't been sick. You haven't gone under the knife or looked death in the face."

He tried to say something, but it didn't come out.

She'd been angry with him then. "Stop thinking about yourself. Stop wallowing in fear of my death. We're all going to die. It's the living that matters. I'm gonna hold and cuddle that baby all I can. Maybe I can leave something of myself with this new life. I'm not going to put off anything that's important. Never again."

He said nothing.

"You're a good man. You've always done your duty. You took care of your parents and provided for your family. You're going to have to find your own way."

When Noreen arrived the following Monday, he was already dressed and had a fire going in both stoves.

"You been plowin'." She wore the same brown sweater as before. Tugging it off, she hung it on a hook near the back door.

"Yes. I'll have ten acres in beets. Been out milkin' this morning."

"Oh, you got your cow back? That's fine. Gives you something to get up for every morning." Noreen reached for a skillet and put it on the stove. "What's her name?"

"Lady. I can't use all the milk. If you want to take some of it, go ahead. Milk for cereal, a little here and there. I don't use that much."

"Thanks. I don't use much milk either, but maybe your daughter Elizabeth could use it. They must buy milk, livin' in town and all."

He hadn't thought of that.

"Why don't you call her? I was thinkin' that Martha and Elizabeth might go through Emma's clothes."

He looked up, startled.

"Now, I know it's hard for you to think about that, but if the girls take anything they want, the rest could go over to the church to help folks. I think Emma would like that."

"Yes, I guess she would."

"Then, okay. Call the girls."

"W-would you call them?"

"No. I don't think it's quite fittin' for me to call." She was stirring some flour and milk for biscuits.

"Well, Emma always..." He let the sentence drift off and went to the telephone. He'd never liked the thing—it rang, it intruded. When you needed it, it was busy.

He rummaged in the drawer for the numbers, found his glasses, and picked up the telephone.

"Number, please," the operator said.

He mumbled Elizabeth's number.

"Nice to hear your voice, Mr. Johnson. Callin' your daughter, then?" the operator asked.

He said nothing, resentful of the inquiry.

When Elizabeth answered, Denver said, "I was wonderin' if you might want to come out and get some milk today."

"Sure, Daddy. I could do that. How are you?"

"Well, I got too much milk."

"Okay, daddy. I'll be out. Anything else?"

"Maybe you could take a look at your mother's clothes with Martha and Noreen. Take what you want."

"Oh. Oh, yes. Have you talked to Martha?"

"No, not yet."

"I'll call Martha and we'll be over soon."

"That'll be all right." Denver hung up. "She's gonna call Martha."

"Come have breakfast. Then you best just get out of here. Don't even come in for lunch. We'll make this as painless as possible." Noreen bent to check on the biscuits.

"Her clothes."

"I know, Denver. It's real personal." She sat down at the table and was silent.

"It's like a toothache, this pain that I feel 'bout Emma bein' gone. It's always there, a dull ache movin' inside that nothin' cures."

Noreen parted a steamy biscuit and spread some butter on it but said nothing.

"Makes me wonder why go on livin'." He hunkered over his breakfast.

"Do you take any joy in seein' her flowers?"

"I s'pose I do."

"How about remembering things you did together?"

"Yes, but that's all over."

"So take that bit of joy, however small, and hold onto it. Be glad for what you had." She paused, then asked, "Do you believe in God?"

"Yes. We went to church, at least some of the time."

"Of course. Most folks do, but do you believe you'll be with Emma again in heaven?"

"I hope so. I'd like to think she's up there now with Harold—not missing him anymore. That's what killed her. Something in her died. It's a terrible thing for a parent to lose a child. It's unnatural."

"I'm sure it is. So, you think Emma is happier than when she was here?"

"Well, I hope so."

"Hoping and knowing, now that's two different things."

"But, how can anyone know for sure?"

"Through faith in Jesus Christ. You know that. Did Emma believe? Was she saved?"

"Oh, yes, 'course. She was a good woman."

"That's not the same. Did she believe?"

"Yes, but she never talked about it much. She loved what she could see. She'd be out there in the garden now, watchin' for little shoots of green." Denver cut the bacon on his plate and took a piece on his fork. When he'd put it in his mouth and chewed it, he went on. "It's harder to really believe in what you can't see."

"Yes. That's where faith comes in."

"S'pose you're right about that. I don't take too much to preachin', though."

"I—I didn't mean to…" Noreen said, uncertain.

"No, and you didn't, but if you're gonna be around here some, well, I thought it best to tell you." Denver looked away, out the window toward something he couldn't see or comprehend, but that still was there: his future.

"Am I gonna be around here some?"

"Well, if you keep on doin' the cleanin'."

"Yes."

"Truth is, Noreen, you make things better when you're here."

"Well, thank you, Denver." She smiled as big as if she'd made a conversion, a shade of pink creeping into her cheeks.

After breakfast, Denver went into his bedroom and opened the closet. Emma's clothes—a half-dozen housedresses and two that she wore to church—hung there. They'd buried her in the one that she wore to the girls' weddings. There was a white one, sprinkled with a variety of yellow flowers, in a kind of soft, swishy material. He pulled it out and carried it to the kitchen where Noreen was washing the dishes.

"Would you like to have this one?"

Noreen turned, took a long look at the dress and a briefer one at Denver.

"Thank you, Denver, but I think your girls should take whatever they want."

"I want to give you this one."

"I know, but I have to say no. No, thank you. If I'm going to be around here some, I don't want you tryin' to make me be Emma."

"No, of course not. Who ever thought of that?"

"Well, maybe you didn't think of it, but wearin' her dress and all would be a reminder."

"I'm sorry. I don't know 'bout these things." He stumbled awkwardly to put the dress away.

It's okay, Denver. He could hear Emma saying this to him, as if she were walking beside him. You've never been through this before. You're tryin'. That's all anyone can expect right now. Her words buoyed him somehow, lightening the weight of his movements through this strange time.

When he returned to the kitchen, he was in control of himself. "I'll be heading out now, Noreen. You'll take care of things with Martha and Elizabeth?"

"Yes. Here—I packed you a sandwich and filled a thermos with coffee for your lunch."

"Oh, well, thank you. Much obliged," he said taking the proffered items and almost smiling.

"I could stay and fix your supper, if you'd like, your not comin' in for lunch and all."

"That'd be right nice, Noreen." He went out the back door, stopping on the porch where he left his boots, a habit Emma had encouraged.

Tools and a wringer washer were there. Next to the washer, two large galvanized tubs stood for rinsing the clothes. He had not used the washer since Emma died. Several times, Elizabeth had taken his wash and returned it neatly folded, but most of the time he wore the same clothes over and over.

When he stepped into the cool morning, the sun was a good way up. He pulled on a hat and worn work gloves while crossing the yard to the tractor. He'd worked the acreage with the big plow that brought up large chunks of earth and worked it again, crisscrossing in the opposite direction. This time, he hooked the smaller plow to the tractor and drove down the lane toward the field.

He passed the broken-down fence again. Each time he did, even when he didn't look at it, he felt a twinge of defeat. The snow was gone. Large boulders stuck out from among the wild grasses and weeds.

As he chugged along, he thought of the women taking Emma's clothes, handling them, and couldn't put that picture away. He reached the end of the lane and turned onto the road for a short distance to where he entered the field to finish preparing the soil where he would soon be planting crops. Water would be coming into the canals and ditches this week, according to a notice he'd received from the water district.

Here's where it goes on. Emma's voice came back to him while he rode the tractor across the field. The sun was high now. Life just keeps on out here. You see all that farmland stretching in every direction and men plowing and planting? Can't you just hear things growin'?

He saw Martha's car going toward the house. She honked, and he waved. A little later, Elizabeth came by. He waved again, and in his mind saw Emma's clothes disappearing.

Those clothes are no use to me now. Emma said in his mind. Martha will take most of the things. Elizabeth will find maybe one nightgown that she thinks still has my smell. She'll bury her face in it and take it home, but she won't wear it.

"Hush. I can't hear anymore."

Be glad you're out here starting something instead of in there, where they're wrapping up the past.

"Hush. I have work to do." He got off the tractor. Taking up a shovel, he cleared the ditches of debris so the water could flow. By the time he'd finished, he was sweating and the muscles along his shoulders ached. Sitting in the shade of the tractor, he took out the lunch Noreen had prepared.

It was quiet out here, though when he paused to listen, the rural air was busy. Every kind of life made its own sounds. Flies buzzed around him. Bees hummed over sweet clover blossoms along the ditch bank.

Other farmers drove past his vision. Trucks with loads of fertilizer went by on the road. Gusts of wind swirled dust clouds.

He didn't miss Emma so much then, and was content for a moment. His thoughts caught up to him, however, and guilt overcame him.

It was nearly six o'clock when he steered the tractor back on the road. Fine dirt covered his clothes and filled the creases in his neck. He was tired all over, but it was a good tired.

Noreen's 1947 Studebaker was still at the house. He remembered that she was fixing dinner. He stopped the tractor and went toward the house.

"You put in a long day," Noreen said as he came in.

"Seems you did too." He saw that she had the table set for two and dinner preparations were under way. "I have Lady to milk and I have to clean up before I sit down to dinner." Tiredness washed over him. He wanted nothing but to sleep.

"We took care of the clothes. Elizabeth and Martha did a right nice job figuring out who would use what. They took everything away."

"Well, that's good then," he said, but inside, he was weary with this new emptiness.

"I think I'll go on now. Here, you see, the stew is at the back of the stove. You can serve it up when you come in. And the biscuits are in the warming oven. There's a salad…" She gestured toward the refrigerator.

"Thank you. I'm very tired." He was standing near the back door, aware of the clean house and the dirt all over him. "I want to pay you."

"Do it next time."

"You sure that's all right?"

She nodded.

"Well…eat dinner before you leave."

"Thanks, perhaps I will."

He reached for the door.

"You all right then?" Noreen asked, looking at him with a kindness he noticed and let sink deep within him. He couldn't yet recognize it as caring on her part or his, because his mind was still full of Emma.

"Just very tired." He flashed on the remnants of Emma being carried out the door like yesterday's newspaper and he knew it was right and proper, but it wrenched at him. He couldn't talk. He went outside.

"I'll see you next week," Noreen said.

He nodded. Back in the barn, he locked Lady's head in place, took a pitchfork, and tossed her some hay. He set the pail underneath her and began the rhythmic pulling of her teats, talking softly as he did, leaning his forehead against the warm brown belly.

The old sounds from all the mornings came back through his head, as if these noises continuously circulated somewhere with the wind and stopped here again on a ceaseless route. The soft low tones brought him a kind of comfort, as well as sadness. He felt tears on his cheek before he knew they were coming, but once he felt that moisture, he let it come. The loosening within him felt right.

That night, he slept well and long.

Chapter Five

Noreen continued her Monday routine. Denver looked forward to the day, lived for it, without admitting that to himself. The echoes of his parents, brothers, Emma, and the children still rang in him. Sometimes he needed to think about the past as if he were adding figures in a book of sums, as if he might better grip the present if he'd accounted for the past.

Though he usually worked outside while Noreen was there, once in a while, he sat in his favorite chair while she finished up in the kitchen and told her some part of the story of his family. The words came natural and easy.

Noreen liked the stories and encouraged him gently with questions, like: "How come your folks happened to settle here?"

"Well, I'm not sure. Guess they'd heard that with irrigation comin' the Boise Valley was a good place to settle. They came from Iowa. Kept movin' and havin' babies. The first child died at five. The second had infantile paralysis at six. Ten children lived; five died at birth or in early childhood. Dad wanted to go west where land, space, and maybe even gold, were abundant."

Denver's father brought the family to Idaho at the end of the nineteenth century, as irrigation was changing the southern Idaho desert of the Boise Valley into a blooming, productive agricultural area. Homesteading 160 acres, Denver's parents gained title to the land by living on it for five years. To buy the property outright would have cost $1.25 an acre.

Denver paused in his recollections to help Noreen find a skillet in the kitchen, noticing how he found her bustling presence reassuring.

"Before I was born, my father hitched up a team of horses and took the oldest boys to the Boise Mountains. They stayed for several days, eating hardtack and dried beef, sawing and chopping trees, and hauling them back to the sawmill where the logs were cut into lumber.

"When they came back, they had the lumber needed to build, the start of this house. It was the best they could do at the time. Had a dirt floor. There was a curtain and a sort of high dresser that divided the space between sleepin' and livin' quarters."

He looked around the room, remembering the changes and the happenings since that time.

"This is where I was born. 1908. In that four-poster bed that I still have. I first slept in a drawer lined with blankets. All the babies did."

Denver told Noreen that after he outgrew the drawer, he slept with three brothers in a wide bed made of wood. The long side was formed by a piece of lumber; the other was the wall. Two shorter pieces of wood nailed the sides together. The frame was held up from the dirt floor with two-by-six-inch pieces of wood. A piece of plywood was the base of the bed. The boys slept under heavy quilts the women had sewn, using any material they could get hold of, backed with denim and stitched without thought to pattern or symmetry.

Denver unburdened himself of the past, handing it on, in a way, to Noreen, who absorbed it in silence for the most part. He wasn't usually an introspective man, but he was looking back now. He didn't stop to question why he was talking more than he ever had, but something in Noreen's quiet, accepting manner allowed him to talk through his life. As he did, a feeling of intimacy grew between the two.

On a morning when Noreen was there, Denver would sit down at the kitchen table, catch sight of the morning newspaper, The Idaho Statesman. This might lead him to tell her that in earlier times there were two local newspapers — The Idaho Statesman and the Idaho Leader. These were their main sources of news, not daily, just whenever his dad went to town and bought an issue. And, the local gossip, as old as anything, flew. Folks talked, of course, and with their words, embroidered a brighter, better, or more exciting life than the one they lived. It seemed like these stories carried on the wind.

"We had to clear the sagebrush when we settled here." Denver shook his head, remembering the wiry, greenish-gray shrubs that spread flat and wide on the arid land. "Before we had crops or cattle, we had to hoe or yank the brush from the dry ground and carry it to the house, where we burned it in the fireplace. Made a hot fire, but didn't last long. My sister, Emily, used to say, 'You know how long it takes for sage-brush to burn? As long as it takes to bring another load to the fire.'"

Denver chuckled, remembering Emily. "She'd snap her fingers to describe how fast Dad acted. He never paused to think first. One time, my brother, Lester was loadin' the fire with sagebrush. He got some of the berries caught in his clothes and they spilled into his oatmeal. Made it very bitter. Terrible really. Lester said he wasn't goin' to eat it. Dad stood over him. 'You eat, boy,' he ordered and he didn't move until every bit of it was gone. None of the rest of us moved, we were so scared. He didn't hit the girls. All the same, his anger was nearly as bad as a whoppin'. I remember, a couple of times…. Suppose the boys wouldn't agree, but I just tried to stay out of his way."

Denver recalled being watched over by his sisters and mother when he was young, growing among the noise and constant family activity. The women sewed clothes and quilts and baked bread in the small oven above the fireplace that was their only source of heat. When he was old enough, he carried water from the creek. Clothes, washed by hand on the small porch at the back of the house, were carried outside and hung on the line to dry.

The Johnson family put every ounce of effort into growing, selling, or using the fruits of their fields. As soon as Denver could pull weeds or collect and carry eggs from the tiny hen house without breaking them, he did.

"Take Denver out with you tomorrow morning. He needs to learn how to milk," his father instructed the older boys when Denver was eight. As far as he could remember, his father never milked the cows, and Denver considered it impossible that he had. His father was too tightly wound to slow enough to meet the pace of the beasts.

Denver recalled Emily saying, "I heard tell that when the oldest ones were born the family had a dining room table, chairs, and real china dishes. By the time we came along, all of that was gone. Dad woulda sold those things when they were movin' and then never found the money to replace them. It wasn't important. He wanted to be rich! So, we ate on chipped, mismatched plates and sat on orange crates."

Lack of success hadn't slowed his father's determination to make big money. One might find a scribbling of numbers on any scrap of paper in the house, calculations the old man had made. His intent was to make money on the land by clearing it. As irrigation made water available, the value would soar. He could sell the land for a good profit and invest in mining. That is where he thought he would make money. He sunk every cent he could squirrel away into mines in Silver City.

"We can get along without . . ." Those words from his father hung over Denver's mind like a creed. (Did the old man think, in order to get to heaven, he first had to pave the streets here with gold?)

When Denver was growing up, the family put aside manual labor and other ambitions on Sundays and went to church, fresh from their Saturday night baths. Denver and the other boys hitched the horses to the wagon. Each wore his Sunday best as he climbed into the wagon and rode the two miles to the Methodist Church in Kuna.

The boys each had a pair of good pants — passed down or made over in most cases — but softer and darker than heavy denim everyday pants. At the first of each month, their mother cut their hair as part of the bathing routine.

Denver pulled out a family picture from the 1920s and showed it to Noreen one Monday. In it, Geneva, one of his sisters, was delicate and pretty. The large white collar she wore, and the way the sun touched her, emphasized her looks. Edith, his older sister, wore glasses. Her head was tilted slightly. Her dark hair added no softness to her face.

"See the way Father's lower lip is thrust forward, his jaw firm. His dark eyes and stern face. That's how I remember him."

He looked at his brothers. "They started going to Los Angeles when they became older and times got tough. We heard tell there was work and money there."

Eventually, Denver started dropping into the café when he was in town. He found reasons to be in that vicinity, enough so that Noreen wasn't surprised to see him and would take her breaks when he was there. He didn't come in wearing his work clothes, but took some effort to be clean and shaven. She'd sit down next to him and ask about his plowing and such.

Finally, one day while Noreen was washing dishes and soap bubbles were floating in the air, he told her about June 17, 1927, the day he married Emma. He was not likely to forget it. She moved into his family home. He thought the situation temporary and promised his young bride that they would be moving before long, living on their own. However, Denver was the youngest child. He felt an obligation to stay with his aging parents to help run the farm.

Emma had no family to speak of — her parents were killed when she was a baby. An unmarried aunt had raised Emma. The sight of the two women working in the garden of the small white clapboard house on the outskirts of Kuna was familiar to most local folks, so ordinary that it almost seemed like the two had emerged from that ground, their faces and arms browned by the summer's sun.

A white picket fence surrounded the house. When Denver had gone to court Emma, he became familiar with the gate in front of the house, the high curved arch above it covered with clematis. Hollyhock and morning glory lengthened out against the fence. Emma's Aunt Bertha had told Denver the morning glory "wanted to take over the place. You can't get rid of it."

After Denver and Emma married and she moved in, his father's temperament did not change, though gout in both feet slowed his movements. He treated Emma, who was soon waiting on him, with a respect reserved for strangers.

"If you wouldn't mind, Miss Emma," his father had prefaced any request, and, "Thank you, Miss Emma." With Denver it was, "Boy, did you get that fence mended? Git on out and git busy!"

"Why doesn't he say thank you to me?" Denver asked Emma once.

"You're kin. He expects it. It's not right, but that's the way it is," Emma said, folding his hand into hers. He would put up with just about anything to be joined with her.

Their first awkward couplings had been ten feet away from where his parents slept. The older couple's snoring was the only promise of privacy the young couple had. The following spring, Harold was born—in the hospital—and less than two years later, Martha.

"Don't see why she has to go to the hospital."

Denver's father objected to the cost. "All my children were born at home."

"Some died at birth. My Emma's gonna be in the hospital and have proper care."

"Let it be, Joseph," Denver's mother said, one of the few times she stood up to her husband.

Ten of the forty acres the family owned was fenced for cattle. Denver, as he had for years, rose at five o'clock each morning. Slipping away from Emma's warmth, he dressed quickly in the dark and added fuel to the nearly dead ashes in the potbelly stove. Taking the freshly washed milk buckets, he walked outside into the silence of the dark morning. The family dog, Rex, a stray they kept for his ability to help lead the cattle, trotted alongside Denver.

Denver began making sounds the cows recognized almost as soon as he left the house, a long-standing practice learned from Basque sheepherders who lived in the area. The sound began with a clicking noise, continued with a guttural sound made by raising the middle of his tongue to the roof of his mouth and pushing upward from deep inside his chest. A bawling utterance was emitted, akin to the mooing of animals.

"Maa—aa—ah," he repeated, liking the sound. He had heard the Basque sheepherders make a higher-pitched "Ye-ee-ee" noise as they herded their flocks through the valley. When his brothers were home, they would make the sounds in unison. Later years, when farmhouses were closer together—most families owned five or ten acres, the man taking a job in town to make ends meet—on the still morning air, he could hear farmers for some distance away making those calls. Sometimes the animals answered or a rooster crowed in another key.

The guttural, primitive tones cleared Denver's head. He felt clean, invigorated and whole as the sun broke open the day like a spilled yolk.

Opening the barn doors on the opposite side from the house, Denver watched as the cows, with Rex nipping at their heels, entered the barn, plodding and stately, milk bags bulging. Hay, pitched into the trough the night before, awaited them. From habit, each cow went to a certain stall and began munching as Denver fixed the piece of wood that held the animal's head in place.

Picking up the milk bucket and a three-legged stool, he pushed his way between the haunches of two cows, sat down near the udders, removed his gloves, and began the rhythmic pulling and squeezing of the teats that brought a steady flow of milk into the bucket.

He talked to the cow he was milking, a sort of rhythmic gibberish that made some link between the animal and the man. Though the number and names—each was called Lady, Tessie, Themilina, or something individual—varied through the years, the routine was constant.

As his parents aged, Emma and Denver took care of their children and his parents, as well as home and land, working long days.

In New York City — an unimaginable place to him — the stock market crashed. The family had no money in it, and Denver did not understand why it mattered, but his father said, "There'll be no money now," with a heaviness as if to say, "or ever."

His father would perhaps have sold the land that was their home at the end of his life but for the Depression, which began soon after the crash and continued through the 1930s. He wrote to his sons in Los Angeles to ask for support in his latest get-rich scheme. His brothers wrote that even in Los Angeles, there were more workers than work. They stood in bread lines.

"I grew up poor," Denver's youngest daughter, Elizabeth, once said at a family gathering when she was a young woman.

"You don't even know what poor is," her uncle hurled back at her. "I begged for milk for my babies."

Here the family had been able to grow their own food. They had a couple of pigs, a small herd of cattle, and some chickens.

While Denver, Emma, and the children lived with his parents, a black-edged envelope would arrive from time to time. Whoever walked down the lane to the mailbox did not rip it open, but carried it back — wondering what drama it contained, sometimes guessing from the postmark.

Denver's mother opened the envelopes, addressed to Rural Route Six, Kuna, Idaho. Emma would stop working during such readings, holding Elizabeth, born in 1932, and watching the infant, William, born a year later. With a look, she silenced the two older children—Harold, born in 1928, and Martha, born in 1930.

Denver's mother would wipe her hands, holding the letter to the light, before slowly loosening the flap and pulling the death announcement from the envelope. One such time, she had turned to her husband. "Your sister, Evelyn, died October 10, 1933. That's over a month ago."

"Does it say the cause?"

"No, but she was older than you. Getting up toward eighty."

"Are you gonna die, Grandma?" His son, Harold, at five, asked.

"We're all gonna die some day, dear." She patted the boy's head fondly. Denver could not recall receiving such a gesture of affection from his mother and ached from the lack of it.

His mother was not harsh like his father, but raising ten children taught her to be miserly in all her ways—never wasting words, time, money, or emotion.

"Just keeping my children alive took all I had," his mother said to Emma one day.

With this death fresh in her hand, his mother looked down to comfort Harold. "We'll all be together again in heaven. Be a good child and you will go there."

Had Harold remembered those words as he lay dying in the sand of Utah Beach in Normandy a little over a decade later?

On a winter morning in 1934, Denver returned from the barn carrying two large buckets of milk. Emma opened the door for him, and he could see that something had changed. "Your mother, Denver." She spoke slowly as if waiting for him to catch up. "She died in her sleep."

He set the milk pails down on a small table in the kitchen. Across the room, his father sat in the rocking chair, head down, arms around it as if shielding himself, still wearing a nightshirt.

Emma took Denver's hand and led him across the wooden floor to the bed where his mother lay. The children were all around, still and wide-eyed.

Maybe she was dead when Denver arose earlier, as he dressed and went out to the morning chores. He wondered about this, though his parents were always sleeping when he rose. He rarely cast a glance in their direction. Still, it shook him inside that she might have been dead and he had not noticed.

"Say something to your father," Emma directed him.

"What?" He glanced toward the old man, who seemed vulnerable for the first time in Denver's memory and separate from the rest of them.

"I'm sorry, Papa."

His father didn't answer.

"Denver will go to the cemetery to arrange for a plot. He will buy a pine box and bring it here. Do you want to pray?" Emma asked her father-in-law.

"Yes." It was a question never answered with "no." He looked at Denver's family as if he did not know them. "Who are these children?"

"They're mine, Papa. Your grandchildren," Denver said.

"Come. We will hold hands and pray with you." Emma gathered her children around, holding baby William and taking Elizabeth's hand, as her father-in-law rose, lumbering and awkward.

Denver knew nothing of what his father said to God that day, but, stunned as he was, he thought he saw the golden dreams of his father in dust on the floor, and that the misery he had put his family through was for nought.

When his father said, "Amen," Emma went to the kitchen and began directing the children in the morning routines. She poured the milk into bottles and put them in the icebox near the back door.

"Come sit down to breakfast," Emma commanded them all. "There is much to be done. We must keep our strength up. Harold, you go with your father, in case he needs anything. Stop by your brother Edward's house, dear. And the minister's. Martha, I'll be needin' you to help clean up around here."

Emma washed and dressed her mother-in-law's body. When Denver and Harold returned with the coffin, they placed her inside the box. As they didn't have a parlor, they set the coffin on a bench near the front door, as far from work and sleep areas as possible.

"Folks will be stoppin' by, Father Johnson," Emma said. "They'll want to pay their respects. Reverend Wilson will help plan the service. You should think about what hymns she would like, and what words ought to be said."

Emma addressed the black-edged envelopes to the family in Los Angeles later. Denver knew about telegraphs and telephones, but no one in the family had a telephone and the cost of a telegraph was out of the question.

The ground was frozen at the time. His mother's body waited in a small building at the cemetery until the grave could be dug in spring.

Through the two days before the service while his mother's body was lying in the house, Denver remained dazed. Family and neighbors came through, solemn and fidgety, with a freshly baked cake or a platter of cookies. Uncertain of the time of day or what to do, Denver simply followed Emma's directions. "Milk the cows. Hold the baby. Speak with your father."

A few months later, while reading a report on the price of silver, his father slumped forward in his chair, dead. The process was repeated.

"How do you get to heaven?" Harold asked, looking at his grandfather in the coffin. "When do you go?"

"I don't know, son. Ask your mother," Denver said.

Wrapping up his recollections, Denver said, "After my parents died, Emma and I took hold of the land and made it ours. It fed us all these years."

"Let's plant some fruit trees, Denver," Emma said as her sights expanded. She rooted into what was now their home and learned to know intimately the patterns of seasons, of weather to be prepared for, and harvests to be gathered.

"We had a neighbor who gave us saplings if we helped pick fruit, so we did, and planted apple, pear, plum, cherry, and peach trees."

Denver, too, was ambitious that their life should go well. He made a contract with the sugar beet factory and planted twenty acres of beets.

Emma wrote letters to Denver's siblings in Los Angeles, keeping up with births and marriages in the family. Some would carry, pour, and smooth cement that would pave and forever change the Los Angeles Basin.

In 1948, Denver's brother Forest died with two pennies in his pocket on a Southern California street. No one, except the family, seemed to care.

It knotted inside Denver that his brother's life had come to nothing. The Los Angeles Police Department, the Los Angeles Times and The Herald found this death too routine to investigate. What Forest's life amounted to was the bits and pieces that his loved ones carried inside — the ear-to-ear smile and the meals, conversations, and laughs they had shared.

He, Emma, and the two youngest children traveled to Los Angeles for the funeral — the only trip they ever took there. William and Elizabeth were teenagers. They sat in the back seat of the car they borrowed for the trip, asking, "Can we go to Hollywood?"

"Your uncle just died and you askin' that question, as if this was a vacation or somethin'." Denver struck out at them.

"We meant after the funeral, Daddy," Elizabeth said in a little voice.

"We didn't even know him," William said. "We never go on vacation."

"Rich folks take vacations. Not farmers. Not folks like us," Denver growled.

"All right, children, that's enough," Emma spoke. "We'll just have to see how things work out, but don't you go talkin' about Hollywood around the family that's mournin'."

Later, they sat with the family while various members pored over the details of this death, combing through it like treasure hunters for a nugget of meaning or sense.

"The police said…"

"He didn't have any money."

"Never fought with anyone that I knew of."

"Why would anyone…?"

"Still, he was out that time of night."

"And, he had been drinking," said his sister, who did not allow drinking of alcohol in her home and would not go where it was served.

On the way home, Emma said, "He had no children. What did he build to leave?"

"Reckon he poured half the pavement in Los Angeles, or seemed to him like he did."

"But pavement doesn't grow anything."

"It doesn't grow crops, but I reckon most of the folks down here don't want to be farmers. Concrete gives you a nice smooth place to park your car."

A cousin took the children for a drive through Hollywood, while the rest of the family sat turning the death over repeatedly, like a puzzle not easily solved. The death struck them full in the face, even as the rest of Los Angeles yawned or drove through it. Denver thought of the endless streets.

"I don't see how folks live so close together," Emma said.

"They don't need space to grow things, just to park their car, so they don't worry about the weather, Emma, or all the sorts of things farmers have to think about."

He remembered the delight in her eyes when they turned onto the lane that led them home.

Christmas in the year of Emma's death was celebrated at Elizabeth and Daniel's house. Noreen was invited to attend with Denver, but she declined, uncertain of how comfortable she would be.

Elizabeth, though heavy with another pregnancy, had every corner of the house glittering — red candles lit on the mantle above the fireplace, a wooden Santa Claus, reindeer, and toy soldiers staged about the house. A nativity scene stood in the hallway near the front door. A large spruce, hung with bright lights and hand-made ornaments, filled the center of the living room.

Where she got the energy, Denver, still in the slough of grief, though slowly pulling back to life, could not imagine.

"The first Christmas is very hard." Martha had said, as did a neighbor. He had repeated the remark to Noreen.

"Just let it happen. Seems like you don't want to anticipate its being difficult. If it is, go with it. Sometimes the only way to get through pain is to experience it," Noreen responded.

Elizabeth, always sensitive, had done everything to make it gay, but she had taken her father aside soon after he arrived at her house. "Now, Poppa, I know how Momma loved Christmas. She would want you to enjoy, but if you feel, at any time, that you want to be alone, or something, you just come in here to our bedroom and close the door. Okay?"

"Well, I reckon it will be all right, but thank you. I'll keep that in mind." Denver patted his daughter's arm as he said this.

Sitting down at the heavily laden table with green candles burning, vegetables in silver dishes, red cranberries in a crystal bowl, the brownish-gold turkey on a platter, and much more, Denver was conflicted, wanting to enjoy, but feeling guilty in taking pleasure.

Enjoy. You are here. You're the lucky one. He knew what Emma would say when they bowed their heads for the blessing. He did not feel lucky — his wife dead in her forties, well before her time.

After dinner, Martha handed her father an envelope. Inside, a note told him that his children had bought him a television. It would be delivered to his house the following day. He had not known what to say, with all of them looking at him, expecting something. "Thank you, don't know as I need one, but . . ."

Martha said, "That's what Momma thought when you brought the radio, wasn't it, Poppa?"

"Yes, yes, you're right. 'Spect things keep a-changin' and we have to keep getting used to it."

When the television was hooked up, he had to admit that he liked watching the old Westerns. Even the news with David Brinkley and Chet Huntley or Walter Cronkite came vividly into the room, making him feel a part of it, somehow. It was 1956, and he wondered what the year would bring.

Early in the next year, Denver spoke to Noreen, haltingly proposing marriage. Denver liked her spunkiness, her matter-of-fact ways. He didn't want to think of life without her.

"I can't be Emma."

"No. Of course not. You could live here. We'd get married, 'course. I'm comfortable with you. You could have your own bedroom. No need to do anything you don't want to." He reddened and looked away. It flashed in his mind that this was a proposal a C-plus person would understand. He was ashamed of himself for thinking of her mother's words and added, "I've grown very fond of you."

He was beginning to move beyond Emma. Noreen, maybe realizing how many marriage proposals she was likely to get, said, "Yes, I'll marry you. We'll just let things happen naturally."

"We'll have to tell the children, I suppose."

"We have to include them."

"We do?"

"Yes. If you want them to accept this, you tell them. I'll make the arrangements from there."

William offered no resistance. Absorbed as he was in his own life in Boise, he was glad his dad wouldn't be alone. He had a job at an insurance company, shared an apartment with two friends, and dated various women — no one regularly that Denver knew of. Denver had been there just once, but he had taken in the Naugahyde bar in the corner and the romantic pictures and lyrics on the 33 1/3-speed long-playing records.

If Elizabeth and Martha objected to their father's marriage, it was not evident: they threw themselves into planning with Noreen. They knew their father would be happier with Noreen in his life. They had seen this over the recent months.

The ceremony took place on April 21, 1956, at Elizabeth and Daniel's house. Denver's family had grown—three children in Martha's family, two in Elizabeth's, with the new baby, Alice, born in February.

Though Noreen had written to her parents in Glenns Ferry, two hours away, her mother had responded by saying they had decided "not to come so far for your second wedding," referring to her earlier, brief marriage. It was one of the few times that he had seen tears glisten in Noreen's eyes.

"She underestimates you. Always has as far as I can tell. You're a fine woman," Denver told her. He thought that again as she stood next to him at the ceremony. He wore a new blue suit and a striped tie his daughters had picked for him. Noreen was unusually subdued that day. She wore a straight butter-yellow dress with short sleeves and a round neck. A strand of pearls that had been Emma's encircled her neck, a gift from Denver.

Afterward, Daniel offered a champagne toast. Elizabeth followed with her own words. "Noreen, you're now a part of our family. We welcome you."

"Yes, we do," Martha added, and William lifted his glass in agreement.

When the minister left, the family of eleven sat down to dinner, first bowing their heads in prayer, then feasting on prime rib carved by Daniel, mashed potatoes, and gravy made from the rich, dark juice from the meat. Noreen's friend, "Aunt Hilda," though retired, had baked a beautiful cake for the pair, but declined their invitation to the nuptials. Homemade ice cream accompanied the cake.

Sally, Martha and Benjamin's four-year-old daughter, sat on a booster seat next to her mother, who tried to keep her daughter quiet and her fluffy peach organza dress clean and in place. She watched Bobbie and Benjy, as well. At six and seven, the boys fidgeted in the suits their parents had bought for the occasion.

Their four-year-old cousin, Bryce, Daniel and Elizabeth's son, hung his head, not looking at the adults at all. He made shapes with his mashed potatoes and shot glances at the other children, watching for an opportunity to tease his cousin, Sally, or to set all the children giggling.

"I'm not getting married when I grow up," Benjy said. "Like you, Uncle Will. You're not gonna get married, are you?"

"Never. Least 'til the right one comes along."

"Me neither," Bryce said. "Not getting married, huh, Bobbie?"

"Nope. I'm gonna be a soldier."

"Me, too," said Benjy. "I wanna fight..." he paused to consider whom he might be warring against, but came up with nothing, so repeated, "I just wanna fight."

"Me, too," Bryce said absently.

"I wanna go with Bryce," Sally said. "Can I go fight with you, Bryce?"

"Don't be silly. Girls don't fight," Bobbie said. "They stay home, have babies, and make dinner."

"Yeah, Sally," Benjy chimed in, "and do what they're told."

Martha looked at her husband when their son said this. Benjamin met her stare briefly. Then they both looked away.

Denver saw the look that passed between the couple. Benjamin still seemed a stranger in the midst of the family. He put in appearances when necessary, but sat awkwardly, while his brother-in-law, Daniel, took charge easily.

"Not me," Sally said. "When I grow up, nobody's gonna be the boss of me!"

Denver and Noreen were to stay in Boise that night and then go on north to Payette Lakes, where they would stay in McCall for a few days. The children had given them the trip. Noreen had arranged for separate rooms.

"I've never seen you so quiet," Denver said when they left. "Are you having second thoughts?"

"No, oh no." She turned to him, resting her hand on his shoulder. "I've never felt so taken in, so accepted. I want to absorb the whole evening into my skin."

She allowed the intimacy between them to grow slowly, as if she understood her just being there, sharing the bathroom, the long days, was a large adjustment.

At the end of August, they took a Saturday off to drive to Boise for the Idaho State Fair. They strolled through sheds with straw covering the floor. Pigs, cows, chickens, goats, and horses raised by members of 4-H Clubs were on display. In other buildings, the best of the harvest was shown — bright yellow squash, white turnips with purple tips, sweet corn, juicy golden peaches, red and yellow apples, and more. Baked goods had been judged. Pies, cakes, and cookies were arrayed along with the ribbons garnered.

They ate barbecued beef and corn on the cob at long wooden picnic tables, and wandered farther into the grounds, nodding and smiling or stopping to chat with people from Kuna whom they saw.

Like teenagers, they played the carnival games and rode the Ferris wheel. When it stopped and they sat at the top, the seat rocking back and forth, Denver put his arm around Noreen. She smiled and took his hand.

The rest of the evening, they strolled hand-in-hand. He wanted her. He thought it would be all right with Emma. He hoped it would be right for Noreen.

When they returned to the pickup, in the darkness, he reached for her. They kissed first slowly, and then long and deep.

Pausing, he stroked her cheek, and whispered that he would like it very much if she came to his bed that night.

She did.

Chapter Six

1970

The first sound Denver heard that morning was Noreen's whistle in the kitchen. He lay there, liking the sound, letting it wash over him. Roosters crowed, their sharp call carrying across the flat farmland. The day sounds started up, the buzz of insects in summer. The day coming into its own.

Once in a while, when he woke in the morning and saw the sun streaming in the window, he thought he should be out in the barn, feeding, milking, and tending the cattle — putting balm on an udder when he saw bleeding from a cut or swelling from a bug bite.

He no longer milked cows, however, and the realization was bittersweet. As a youth, he hadn't wanted to get up and go out into the dark, cold mornings, but his father had said to go. He went. Then his own children came and had to be fed. By then, the early morning rituals had become a part of him, part of the life that he and Emma shared.

Now, however, Denver and Noreen used little milk. She did not take to making cottage cheese and butter the way Emma had. The Carnation Company no longer found it profitable to pick up one or two cans from small producers, so, over ten years ago when Lady, his last cow, died, Denver quit milking.

At sixty-two, he was vigorous and healthy. He carried no extra weight on his body. A twinge of arthritis in his hands from time to time reminded him that he was aging. As a child, he would roll a snowball over the new whiteness, turning and packing the snow as long as he could move it, or until it fell apart from the weight. Memory was like that, packing and carrying life's happenings forward so the weight increased with age. So much of his life was over.

Still, there was this day, and nothing wrong with it either, Noreen's contented whistling told him. He got up and began dressing. No more milking. They bought dairy products at the supermarket.

"This cottage cheese isn't so fresh. It doesn't taste as good as homemade," Denver said the first time he tasted it.

"Do you want to go back to milking?"

After that, he ate it and said nothing. Eventually it tasted all right to him, though if the subject came up—it rarely did—he would say, "Nothin' like that homemade cottage cheese that Emma used to make."

"Grandma, please make cocoa when I come," Alice, Elizabeth's daughter, would say to Noreen. Denver was glad for the request. Powdered hot chocolate was a poor replacement.

Alice was born after Emma's death and had always called Noreen "Grandma." Lithe and fair-haired, Alice took gymnastics and did flips across the grass in the summer when she visited — her long hair flying. So light and airy were the young girl's body and spirit that both seemed to soar naturally.

By the time Denver came to the kitchen that morning, Noreen had turned up the heat, started brewing in Mr. Coffee, and awakened the place. She was outside, walking to the end of the lane to get The Idaho Statesman, something she did every morning, year round. In winter, she donned warm boots and a heavy coat for the half-mile walk.

Looking out the window, he saw her striding down the lane, the light blue sweater she wore melding into the sky beyond. He smiled. She would be opening the door soon. Her short, blonde hair was brushed softly around her face, which was a little plumper than when she started coming here. It had been too thin, then. He hadn't thought her pretty in the beginning, only necessary.

"You can drive to get the paper," Denver told her.

"No. The walk wakes me up. I look across the valley at the farms and the trees, watch how things change with the seasons, and beyond, the mountains. I like seeing for a long, long way."

"Emma used to talk that way about the land."

"The footings have been poured on the corner lot across the lane. A house will be goin' up soon."

She set the paper on the table, pulled off her sweater, hung it on a hook near the door, and turned to pour coffee.

"With new building creeping closer, I wonder how long we'll be able to see across the valley. We'll always see the mountains, of course, but when houses are built near, that blocks the view and…I don't know, somethin' else," said Denver.

"I know. For me, the land quiets body and soul. I've never heard you talk about the land that way, though—what it does for the spirit," said Noreen.

"The land has always been necessary, so I haven't thought about it like you do. This is the only place I've ever lived. What do I know? Spent very few nights anywhere else. I didn't choose this life or this place. It just happened. I 'spose I take the land for granted, though I like hearing you talk about it."

"Still, we aren't getting any younger. The day will come when we decide this land is too much to take care of."

"Oh, I hate the thought of moving to town." When Denver said this, he thought of his four brothers who had died. After the last one, his sister in Los Angeles had proposed that the remaining siblings sign the property rights for the farm over to Denver.

"Seems to me," Emily had said, running her nervous, work-worn hands through her thinning hair, "like Denver has worked the land all these years. I think, maybe, it ought to be his. What do the rest of you think?"

"I imagine that'd be all right." They'd all agreed.

They gathered, as they always did when someone died, as if you had to take that final step to get your family's attention. There, they told the family tales, looked at the young children, whose bodies were as unwilling to be still as the older ones were to move.

One morning, the telephone rang while Denver and Noreen were eating breakfast. Denver listened automatically for two long rings, though they heard only their own ring now and shared the line with just one other party.

Noreen picked up the phone on the wall, a long cord stretching from it, so she could talk and walk about the kitchen. If Martha called or Elizabeth, she chatted with them while emptying the dishwasher or wiping the counter clean.

"William, how are you?" She asked and then listened. "Okay. Here's your father." She handed the telephone to Denver.

Denver's younger son, William, had moved his family when the company he worked for offered him a promotion if he took a job in Southern California. He and his wife, Susan, had two children—Sarah, now twelve, and ten-year-old Ronald.

"Hi Dad," William said. Denver couldn't remember the name of the town where they lived. It was forgettable—"La" something or other. The two chatted briefly, before William said, "We're planning our vacation. Thought we might come up there in July. What do you think?"

"Fine. Be good to see you. Do you want to send Ronald early? Sarah came a couple of years ago. Was she ten?"

"Yes. That would be about right."

"Maybe it's time for Ronald."

"I think so. We've been talking about that. He will be thrilled to fly up there by himself. And, he likes being on the farm," William said.

"I know. Not like his father." Apparently, William never gave a thought to running the farm though, as a child, he had followed his mother around the garden, talking about soil and growth. With William's stocky build and large "farmer hands" and his intuitive sense of the weather, Denver had thought he might return to the farm. He'd saved the herd once when he was ten by insisting that they bring the cattle into the barn that night, certain that the storm would be worse than predicted. The blizzard that hit had left cattle bewildered, lost, and dead all over the valley, while theirs were safe inside.

"Right. But, he never lived on it." William's voice thickened slightly. It was the deaths, Denver thought, that pushed William away — Harold, when William was ten, and his mother, when he was twenty-one. His grandparents had died there within a year of William's birth, and Denver wondered if those losses, too, were somewhere in his son's memory.

"True. How's your work?"

"Fine, been travelin' quite a bit. I get tired of that and so does Susan, but when the company says go, I go. They pay me well. You'll have to come down and see our new house and pool. Come down in the winter when it's cold up there."

"Perhaps we will." He and Noreen had gone to Southern California to visit William's family about five years before, but the dizzying number of freeways, traffic, and people made them glad to return home.

"Ronald plays basketball, so you could see his games in the winter."

"I'd like that. You have a hoop for him on the garage?"

"No, that's not allowed in our neighborhood, but he practices at school."

"That's good, but seems a shame you can't play one-on-one with him."

"I know it sounds strange, especially to someone who lives in the country, but here, houses are close together, so when we and all our neighbors are restricted--we can't have a boat or a trailer setting out front and we can only paint our house certain neutral or natural colors—it makes some kind of sense. Anyway, we agreed to it when we bought. Preserves the value of the house. If someone moved in across the street and painted their house purple, well, we might not be able to sell our house when we needed to."

Denver responded, "Some people do use wild colors here. I don't like it, but I figure it's their business."

"I know. Houses are so close together here. We have a quarter of an acre. That's considered a good-size lot," William replied.

"So, we would have 160 houses on this property if it were divided that way," Denver calculated.

"Hard to think of, isn't it, Dad? Farms down here have been divided just like that. There's no end in sight."

"Yep. Well, listen, put Susan on. I'll say hello and then put Noreen on. They can arrange the details. We're always home, so it's your schedule we have to work around."

"You don't think about doing some traveling?"

"Most of my life I couldn't afford it. Now things are a little easier. Just never been used to traveling."

He and Noreen had worked hard after they married in 1956. They planted all of the land except the area around the house, the sheds, and the barn. Noreen threw a shovel over her shoulder and strode along the ditch bank, opening a channel here and closing one there. Not a delicate woman, she worked in the fields hard as any man.

"Well, we'll talk about it when we're up. Oh, we got a letter from Bobbie."

"Good. We hear occasionally and, of course, we watch the news." Bobbie was in Vietnam, and the presence of his grandson there cast a shadow over all else in their lives. Bobbie had married Debbie at the county courthouse a couple of months before he left. Denver and Noreen met the new bride when they attended a reception at the home of Debbie's parents.

"Yes, well, we'll talk about that too when we're there, I'm sure. Here's Susan. Oh, and I love you, Dad."

"You too, son. You take care, now, you hear?" He greeted his daughter-in-law and handed the telephone to Noreen.

Pouring himself another cup of coffee, Denver sat down at the table while Noreen talked, wondering idly if his son ever felt hemmed in by the requirements of his life and if his grandson, Ronald, would consider farming. Not that they could afford to pass the land on—it would probably have to be sold at some point so Noreen and he could afford to live in town.

From the time they got married, Noreen studied agriculture and the markets—as neither Denver nor Emma had. In winter, she drove to the library and came home with books on weather, planting, harvesting, and investing. They had two reclining chairs. Noreen would make a fresh pot of coffee after lunch. With a full cup next to her, glasses resting low on the bridge of her nose, she sat reading in the recliner, marking things she wanted to save, making notes on the brochures published by the U.S. Department of Agriculture. Everything that pertained to farming and the financial markets in the newspaper got her attention.

Early on, she had tried to engage Denver in discussions about what she was learning. "Wine is the drink of the future. Perhaps we should plant a vineyard. What do you think?"

"Never planted grapes. Don't know the first thing about 'em."

"Oh, but I do. I've read about them." Noreen said, still recognizing that what she had read might not be sufficient to make the costly transition to grapes.

Having led a physically active life in which there was often no energy left by the end of the day and little chance to study or indulge his imagination in novels, Denver wasn't fond of reading. In the evenings, he watched television. Noreen paid little attention except to the news. He soon relied on her and let her lead in such decisions. As Emma had led in their life together, Noreen now did in a different way. Denver never minded; rather he was grateful that she took the interest. Noreen insisted they join the Grange, a farmer's association, not for the social aspects, but for the information they could gather.

After a winter of planning, they went to the fields to prepare the soil and plant the crops. Though she paid little attention to flowers and planted only a few vegetables, she made sure every ditch bank was mowed clean of weeds. Crops, once planted, were kept well irrigated, fertilized, and weed free—Noreen and Denver walking the rows with a hoe to take out any offender. The company representatives who bought their crops soon knew that anything from the Johnson farm would be of the highest quality, whether it was sugar beets, soybeans, or seed corn.

Each year, they updated a part of the house and the farm equipment—adding central heating, the latest and best plowing implement, or a fresh coat of paint for the house and the barn. Led by Noreen, they invested some money for their future.

Denver wished that his father could see the farm now, at its best. Noreen deserved much of the credit for that.

When Noreen hung up the telephone, she turned to picking up the breakfast dishes. "It's settled, then. Ronnie will fly up a week before the rest of the family drives. He'll be here at the end of June, so they'll all be here for the Fourth of July. Let's see if Martha's and Elizabeth's families can come for a picnic that day. Be quite a thing to have all the families together. It's been some time."

"That would be something. Benjy may ship out to Vietnam before then." Denver had no heart for this war. His father would have said go, and his own generation said so, too. He wondered what Harold would have said, or Bobbie, now that he was there, waking up mornings in the rice paddies of Vietnam where it was so difficult to tell who the enemy was.

"We should invite Debbie, though we don't see her much. Wonder how much she hears from Bobbie." Thinking of Bobbie's wife, she added: "It's good that she didn't get pregnant. They were only married, what, two months before he left."

Martha called when she got a letter from Bobbie. Between the various communications, they were able to track his company's movements somewhat.

"It's the pictures, the TV that makes people hate this war. Oh sure, we saw a newsreel every once in

awhile during the big one, but nothing like this,"
Noreen shuddered, picturing explosions and deaths
she'd seen on television.

"I still remember Emma's face when Harold left.
It's just as hard for Martha." Denver's face twitched in
an effort to contain the sad memory.

"Do you think Bobbie should have gone or that
Benjy should go?" Noreen asked.

"I was proud when Harold went. I'm worried
about Bobbie and, course I will be about Benjy. I
guess I keep hoping Martha's life will get better, but
it never seems to. She can be proud of Sally as a good
student and of her sons for serving their country. But,
I worry about her. I'm afraid for her. She tends toward the dark side, as if that's where she fits."

"Oh, I hope you're wrong," Noreen stared out the
window, before adding, "Where is pride for this war?
Have you seen it?"

"No, no I haven't. The country's so split. Bobbie
was drafted. Harold chose to go." Denver saw the two
boys in his mind, though war had kept them from
ever seeing each other.

"But do you think Benjy should go?" Noreen persisted.

"What choice does he have? We don't have money
or connections. I've always thought a man should be
willing to fight and die for his country. Still, I don't
want them to go. Not Benjy." Denver's brow furrowed as he felt the weight of these wars, these lives.

"Martha's children are at odds over the war. Sally
is against it, you know."

Denver shook his head. "What does an eighteen-year-old girl—even a smart one—know? What has the world come to that anyone is paying attention to what these kids think?" He shook his head. "What awful choices they have to make!"

"It's come to television and information. To the United Nations and Eisenhower's domino theory. Life is simpler when everyone agrees on what's right or wrong, but that hasn't happened in this war. I think the world has changed. It's become more complicated." Noreen said with a sigh.

"I'm not sure it's for the better," Denver commented quietly. He knew she had a point, but his experience made him feel that what had been done in the past was how things should be done. Older people making the rules; younger ones following.

Silence took both of them then, as if the questions were too much, the results too unknown.

When the Vietnam War grew large and controversial, the pictures that previously had been newsreel footage on rare occasions or a vivid photograph in the newspaper came surging into his home on the television continually. It was too much.

He turned away from his thoughts and back to Noreen: "I don't know. I think that when Harold went to war, he saw guns and glory and the American flag."

"These young men see horrible death and ask themselves what is this for," said Noreen. "I wonder what Bryce will do. He's near draft age."

"You're right. He may have to go. Seems impossible he'll be eighteen." As Denver said it, a skittering of fear went through him for this mild-mannered second child of Elizabeth and Daniel.

"I never had any children of my own, but I can imagine how hard it would be. Your family…"

"My family is your family. Why, William's kids, Sarah and Ronnie, never knew their grandmother, nor did Elizabeth's Alice for that matter. You are grandmother to them. Bobbie and Benjy, even Sally, remember Emma a little. You — you saved my life, you know."

"Oh, don't be silly."

"I couldn't have done it. I was lost. All those connections with my kids and grandkids — you oiled them. You smoothed the way."

"I'd probably still be working at the café had you not come along. I like being part of your family."

Denver remembered a week in 1956 after the State Fair. With canning season upon them, Martha and the children came over to help pick the fruit. Taking pails, baskets, and every other container they could find, the family went to the orchard. Denver carried a ladder. Noreen brought a couple of step stools.

The trees that had been mere twigs, when Emma had planted them twenty years before, were now tall. The branches, heavy with fruit, stretched wide and reached high, forming a canopy of shade. Underneath the trees, long green grass grew.

"Children, I want you to pick up the fruit on the ground first. If it's soft or rotten, throw it in here." Noreen indicated a certain bucket. "Be careful where you step."

"Can I climb the tree? I wanna get up in the tree," said Bobbie.

"Me, too," Benjy and Sally said together. (And, now, he reflected on how these children who had been so young were facing the realities of war. A shiver went through him.)

"Pick up what's on the ground first. Then we'll see." Martha laughed. "That's what my mother used to say to me."

"She loved this orchard," Denver said. "'Course, it's always cooler here than out in the fields blazin' with sun."

"It's protected, and the fruit — look at this peach, must be four inches across. We should have taken it to the fair."

The orchard was next to the house, on the opposite side from the barn and other sheds, just beyond the garden. Noreen stooped over, working the ground with the children. When she found a peach that was near perfect, she pulled out a pocketknife and cut it open, handing large slices to the children, then to Denver and Martha. They ate, with the juice dribbling down their chins and onto their hands.

"How's Benjamin?" Noreen asked Martha. "We don't see him too often."

"Daddy's always working or sleeping," Sally answered. "He's not with us, like Momma."

"He's busy all right," said Martha.

Denver heard an edge in her voice. He had never been comfortable with Benjamin, who seemed to be always following his life rather than leading it, a course Denver knew was not unlike that which he had taken.

"Now can we climb in the trees?" Bobbie asked when most of the ground fruit was collected.

"Go for it!" Denver said. The kids did, loving the off-the-ground feeling.

By 1965, Noreen and Denver did the picking and canning on their own, though often sharing some of the fruit with the children. One day, they loaded baskets of fruit into the car and drove to Martha and Benjamin's house.

They didn't know just whom they would find at home. Martha worked as a clerk at J.C. Penney's. Bobbie had a job setting pins at the bowling alley. Benjy mowed lawns and did odd jobs, trying to save money to buy a car. Sally helped her mother with the house and went to summer school.

The brick house sat on a two-and-one-half acre site, set well back from the road, designed for families who wanted a garden, a couple of cows, and maybe a horse.

"The folks that live here aren't farmers and they aren't exactly city folks, either. They're a little of both," said Noreen. "Their kids will live in town."

"Looks like no one has mowed the lawn for awhile." Denver saw, to the left of the house, a couple of junk cars parked where they had been for a long time. Weeds straggled through the motor of an old Studebaker. Benjamin owned a small car repair and body shop on Caldwell Boulevard. "Cars and football, seems like that's all he cares about."

"Well, maybe not all."

"What do you mean?"

"I think he likes women."

"Do you know something 'bout his doins'?" Denver didn't want the answer. He had avoided this, hoping that the stories were not true. In Kuna, a person earned a reputation—deserved or not, sometimes from a family incident or peculiarity, and seldom lived it down. Though Denver was not taken with Benjamin, he had tried to be fair. In his youthful exuberance, Benjamin drove too fast, partied hard, and drank beer when he was under the legal age.

His courtship of Martha had been stormy. One night after he dropped Martha off, driving back through town, he had "run into a couple of buddies," as he put it. Six young people had gone out to Dry Lake to spin wheelies, and the car had flipped, pinning two of the six young people underneath. Though both had survived, their injuries were severe, and Benjamin's rowdy image was set with the locals.

"Martha said he doesn't always come home at night," said Noreen.

"So there's clearly trouble." They parked the car.

Thirteen-year-old Sally came out the front door and waved at them. When she reached the car, she hugged Noreen and then her grandfather. Her body was straight and skinny, but sturdy with broad shoulders—not small boned. Her hair was Emma's, thick and full and reddish brown.

"Hi. We brought some fruit over for you," Noreen said.

They carried the ripe peaches and pears into the house.

"The house looks nice. You're a big help to your mother. Do you want to go have some lunch with us? We were on our way into town. We're going to stop by Lizzie's and then go to the café."

"Thanks, I'd like to, but I have to babysit at the neighbors in half an hour."

"Are you saving for anything special?" Denver asked.

"Yes. I'm gonna go to college, Granddad. I'm not gonna be like these kids around here who grow up not knowing what they want to do or be. Like my brothers and my dad...worthless."

"I bet we can find a bite here." Noreen said as she led them into the kitchen. She pulled out a loaf of bread and looked around. "What do you have for sandwich fixins'?"

Denver sat down at the chrome-and-Formica table.

"Why do you feel that way about your father?" Denver asked.

"He's cheatin' on mom. She works hard and Bobbie and Benjy aren't exactly easy for her. She has to be both parents. Dad's just never been around much. I'm never getting married! Why does she take it?"

"You marry for better or worse. In our family, I don't think there's ever been a divorce. You make the best of it. I've been fortunate. I've had two good marriages. I wish your mother had had one," Denver said.

"Do you talk to your mom about this?" Noreen asked.

"No. She won't talk about it. I said to her, 'Why didn't Daddy come home last night?' She said, 'Oh, he must have fallen asleep at work and slept on that couch in the back.' Bobbie was out and he said Dad's truck wasn't at the shop. He saw it at the Black Cat Lounge. When he comes home, there'll be a big fight. I hate it."

"Does he hit her?" Denver hated asking the question, pondering the possibility, loathing the painful silence that followed.

"Sometimes, but not in the face where you'd see it." After saying this, Sally cried and Noreen wrapped her arms around the young body.

"Does...does he ever hit you?" His voice had gone guttural, reaching into a deep part of himself. Her words had loosened old volumes of anger in him, a stored library of striking out, the source of which was partly his father, but where did his father get it? Someone struck him, and before that, back, and back.

Before she could answer, a screen door banged. Sally moved quickly, wiping her eyes. Benjamin, entered the kitchen, looked around, and saw his daughter's tear-stained face.

"What's goin' on?" he asked, looking from one to another. He planted his feet wide apart with his hands on either side of his waist, so the dirty fingernails and calloused hands stood out. His plaid, western shirt with pearly buttons stretched tight over his swelling gut. His Levis were soiled and worn.

Denver rose uncertainly.

Noreen spoke quickly. "We were about to have some lunch. Sally and I are fixing some sandwiches. Tunafish. Hungry?" She paused and looked toward Benjamin briefly, then went on, "We stopped by with some peaches. We've been pickin' and you know how fast they ripen. Sally said she has to babysit soon, so we just thought we'd have a bite before she leaves. Come, Sally, let's get the table set. What about something to drink? Let's see." She opened the refrigerator, continuing to talk as if she could not stop — could not bear what might come when she did.

"I think I better go." Sally rushed from the room.

"You should eat." Noreen's voice rose with a quiver. "She doesn't eat enough. See how thin she is."

The girl was gone.

"Sit down, you two," Noreen said.

The day was hot, the air still, the silence wide. Benjamin took large gulps of milk between the bites of sandwich, swallowing loudly and bringing the glass back to the table with a whack.

"How you and Martha getting along?" Denver muttered, finally.

"Fine."

"No problems?"

"Huh-h. You know any marriage that doesn't have problems?"

"If you ever hit her…"

"Yeah, what if I do? I don't like her workin.' Makes people think I can't support my family. I'm the man. She's s'pose to do what I tell her."

"Don't hit her…or the children," Denver said, his voice low, gruff, catching deep in his throat.

"It's better to talk things out," Noreen said, wanting to mitigate the tension.

"Talk, talk, talk. That's all you women want. I'm through talking,'" Benjamin snarled.

"Hitting doesn't solve anything," said Denver. "It's wrong! You know that!"

"No! I'm the man! She has to know who's boss."

"What kind of a boss is that? Just proves you're bigger and meaner." Denver had never been close to his son-in-law, but on family occasions Benjamin had been polite, not rough and angry as he was now.

"We best be going," Denver said to Noreen.

"Yes, I'll just do these dishes."

"Leave them. It's time for us to go."

Benjamin continued to sit, looking away toward some point Denver could not see. Perhaps the younger man was staring at disappointment, at something tenuous, even tender, some level of respect that was lost on this ordinary day, and how unrecoverable that loss was.

Denver felt an emotion between pity and sadness. Things had been said that could not be unsaid. They could no longer be a polite family together. Benjamin,

Martha, and the children coming over in fresh clothes with their faces washed and their hands clean. These family occasions kept some fiction alive that was now pierced, deflating the air and the spirit. Somehow, Denver thought, this gave rise to awful possibilities. The happy family was not entirely an image. As long as it was portrayed, some part of it was true. That image was now gone. Denver wondered what was to become of Martha's family.

Benjamin said nothing as Denver and Noreen started toward the door.

"If counseling would help, that is…make you and Martha get along better, we will help any way we can," Denver said, turning to Benjamin.

"Tell some shrink my problems! Forget it. Stay out of our business. Don't come nosin' around here." He didn't look at the two, but stretched his legs out under the table and crossed one over the other, as if he were relaxing, slipping into this new meaner skin, getting used to it.

Later, after Benjamin and Martha divorced, Noreen said, "We shouldn't have gone to their house that day. That started it all."

"What do you mean? It started long before that."

"Yes, but our being there brought it out in the open. So, then we had to do something. We had to protect Martha and Sally mostly. Bobbie and Benjy could take care of themselves by then."

"My father would strike the boys, but never the girls, and certainly not his wife. I thought Benjamin wouldn't either."

"Many men do." The night after they had been at Benjamin and Martha's, Noreen had told him—the only time she mentioned it—that her first husband had struck her often.

"How could you take it? What did you do?"

"I told my mother. She looked at me like a pest she thought herself rid of and said, 'You made your bed. Now lie in it.' Nothing changed until Aunt Hilda noticed some bruises and asked me about them. When I told her, she said, 'Young lady, you aren't going back to him. You stay in my back room. You don't deserve to be beaten up.' And I did stay there for a time. Lucky for me, he was in construction work and he got a job in Idaho Falls and forgot all about me. Signed the divorce papers without question. We didn't have anything to fight over."

"I can't understand how a man hits a woman or a child. And Noreen, didn't we help Martha like your Aunt Hilda helped you?"

"We intended to, but I don't know. Is Martha happier now? You know, she lost face with a lot of people in town. We did what we had to do, but I'm just sayin' sometimes people don't want rescuing. With me, I was younger and had no children, and I think the beatings were more severe."

"And Elizabeth..." Denver began.

"She is kind to her sister, but even that is hard for Martha. Lizzie's life seems to float along so smoothly. I think Martha sees herself as a failure by comparison."

"She shouldn't compare."

"But children do. And Lizzie is right here for other folks to see. William is successful, but he's off in California," Noreen commented.

"I don't think she was ever jealous of William. You don't think that Martha is very happy, then?"

"No, I don't. Do you?"

"I suppose not, though in time things may get better. I hope so."

"I do too, of course."

"How can we help?"

"Love her, care for her. Let her know we don't think she has failed."

"I wonder why she has more problems than the other two. Seems like she has always given more than she got back. She took care of the others and her mother when Emma was sick," Denver pondered.

"It's hard to say why things work out the way they do for folks. We just have to do the best we can, I s'pose," Noreen concluded.

Chapter Seven

In the spring of 1970, Sally Samuels received a full scholarship to attend Stanford University, putting to rest the words her brothers had often used when they referred to her as a "dumb girl," using the two together as one would say "blue sky."

"Maybe they did her a favor in the long run," Noreen said. "She's gonna prove them wrong. That's what drives her."

"Maybe, but it wasn't a favor…and they will be the last to give her any credit. Just as your mother has never seen your worth, so it sticks in your craw," Denver responded.

"Yeah, you're right about that. I s'pose it's the way their father treated their mother—that's where they get it."

"Both the women in my life have been smarter than me and, far as I'm concerned, so much the better for me." As Denver said this, he turned and smiled at Noreen, glad for the warmth and comfort they had in each other, even as he remembered Emma, her love of their children and the land, the energy she brought to what she cared for.

"Oh, I don't know about that. I bet you figured out that if you praised me, I'd study the books on farming and you wouldn't have to," Noreen teased.

"And you fell for it."

Sally's brother, Benjy, lived with his mother and worked at his dad's auto shop. His grandparents saw him only on family occasions.

"He goes out most evenings," Martha told them. "He doesn't have a steady girlfriend. Hangs out at some bars or drags Main. I hope he isn't using drugs. A friend of his was arrested for drugs just last week. Benjy is the me-too kind."

"Does he help out at home?" Denver asked.

"You're kidding."

"He should…" Denver stopped, his mind flying backward to his boyhood when he was expected to take care of his parents and work on the farm. His children were all eager to be out and on their own. Benjy was neither willing to help nor eager to leave.

Benjy drove a blue-and-white 1956 Chevrolet Bel Air, which he had made into a "low rider," so the body of the car sat almost on the ground, bouncing and scraping the pavement or dirt when it hit a bump.

Shorter than Bobbie and less handsome, Benjy, at five-foot-eight, was skinny and pale, with long brown hair pulled back in a ponytail. He wore tattered Levis and white cotton T-shirts, one sleeve rolled up to hold his cigarettes.

Martha continued to work at J.C. Penney, where she had become a supervisor. Denver wondered if Martha would keep the house after Sally went away to college. Sally would not be back much—that was plain to her grandfather. She had big plans and wide horizons.

Both Sally and her cousin Bryce graduated that spring, in a ceremony held at the Kuna High School football field. Bryce would be attending the University of Idaho at Moscow, in Northern Idaho.

Noreen had suggested that they invite everyone to their home after the ceremony. She insisted on including Benjamin, though Denver had objected, as had Sally and Martha.

"He's still her father," Noreen told Denver and Sally. "And he's not all bad."

Sally had looked far away, as if trying to see something not in her sight. "Sometimes I feel as if I never had a father. He never hit me, you know. He hit the others—Mom, Bobbie, and Benjy—not so often, but you knew he might. 'I'll give you what-for' he would say, and he would clench his hand and shake his fist. But, that was when he was home—he was gone so much of the time. Mostly I remember him gone, so we looked to Mother for everything."

"I know, dear." Still, Noreen held onto people and saw value that others overlooked, though she was not blind to their faults. She went to church, not every Sunday, but she was deeply religious, not in a talky or showy way. She just was. It was a religion not of church but of soul.

On the day of graduation, Elizabeth came in the early morning to Denver and Noreen's to bring food, flowers, and other decorations, to create a festive atmosphere.

The women filled vases and glass jars with blue iris, deep red roses, greenery, bluebells and asters. They hung a banner congratulating the graduates.

"It's a day to be proud, Papa." Elizabeth said as she snipped the end of an aster. "These two, Bryce and Sally! No telling what Sally's going to do."

Denver understood why Martha thought everything came easy to Elizabeth. While Martha struggled to pay the bills and keep her children in order—Benjy was a handful and Bobbie a worry—her sister's house was always in order, her life intact, her flowers blooming on schedule, and her husband responsible and kind.

Elizabeth took it upon herself to care for others. She had taken Sally under her wing when her parents divorced and her mother was busy. Elizabeth loved flowers, music, and the theatre, but she worried about the war and education. She had been president of the local PTA and active in the League of Women Voters.

Elizabeth awakened Sally's political and ethical conscience. "Little Lizzie," as Harold had called her so long ago. Lizzie, of the sweet face and easy manner, engendered a curiosity in Sally. Lizzie brought her niece books, walked and talked with her through town, or sat with her in the garden. Lizzie cared. Sally sopped up the attention like a sponge and rose to the challenge.

"We shouldn't be there," Elizabeth said to Sally and her own children. "We should not be in Vietnam."

The week before graduation, Elizabeth took her children and Sally to a demonstration in Boise. Noreen spotted them in television coverage.

"Come here, quick," Noreen had called to Denver.

He'd seen the placards, "Bring our sons home," "No more war," and "Hell no, we won't go."

"Why doesn't she stay home, mind her own business?" he asked, fiercely, perhaps because he knew what he couldn't articulate, which came in Noreen's next words: "This is her business—Bobbie over there. Benjy drafted. Young Bryce likely to go."

"I never saw the like." Denver mumbled, thinking how it was hard to understand the changes that kept coming at them, dust flying continually on the wind.

Daniel's parents had apparently not been pleased to see Elizabeth and the children demonstrating on television. Daniel received an angry call. "Couldn't he keep his wife in place?"

"Daniel wasn't very happy with me either," Elizabeth told Noreen.

It wouldn't be easy for Daniel to be angry with Elizabeth—it was her way. She was pretty and smiled easily. She was neither harsh nor mean and rarely confrontational. She was charming—what had Daniel to go up against all that? He was her husband. He supported her. She created a life for him—a nest with warmth, comfort, and laughter.

"Does Daniel support the war?" Noreen asked Elizabeth.

"Well, yes, though he has doubts. He didn't object to my going to the rally. He knows by now that I have a mind of my own—though sometimes, I'm sure, he wishes I didn't. If it hadn't been for my being on television, he wouldn't have minded. But, when other people saw me—his parents, people at the bank—that's what made him uncomfortable."

"He's thinking of his place in the community," said Noreen.

"And I'm thinking of Bryce turning eighteen next month. I can't bear the thought of his going to Vietnam. At least when Harold went, he chose to go, even lied about his age so he could go. Maybe he just craved excitement. I remember sitting in his room talking the night away before he left—all of us kids. His eyes were shiny. I remember it so clear."

Her hands rested against the counter and she looked out the window, though Denver thought she did not see the fields and flowers. Her thick full hair was tied back under a scarf, and her blue eyes were liquid and full with what they saw.

"The four of us had gone swimming in the canal. You know, it was one of those very hot days. We walked barefoot down the lane to the water. Harold's spirits were so high; it seemed like he would fly. He laughed at everything and teased Martha about her boyfriend—she had started seeing Benjamin. 'Does he kiss you, Martie?' he asked. 'Do you French kiss? I saw that hickey on your neck.' Martha reddened and then he threw water at her and she threw it back at him until she wasn't mad anymore. It got late and I said we should go home, that Momma was preparing a special meal. Harold didn't want to leave. He kept diving in just one more time.

"William said to his brother, 'You could get killed.' Just like that and I saw a look go through Harold, just lasted a split second, he wouldn't let it stay longer, as if he had heard something he hadn't understood before, but then, he dived again and when he came up he said, 'I'll get the Jerry before he gets me.' He had to believe that, had to keep the excitement going. That's why we were in his room late that night. Talking and talking. He couldn't sleep.

"With Bryce nearing draft age, I think of Harold a lot. I know how much Momma hated his going, but what could she do? He wanted to go. Everybody believed in that war. This one is different."

"How?" Her father asked.

"The objectives are less clear. We were attacked in World War II. Vietnam is not a threat to the United States," Elizabeth said.

"Communism is, though, with its plan to take over the world, little by little, country by country," Noreen said.

"But we are destroying the country we seek to save," Elizabeth said.

"You have to draw the line somewhere. The Commies got Eastern Europe when Stalin outsmarted Truman at those conferences," said Denver.

"Yes and they control much of Asia. He's right. You have to stop them somewhere. How about Cuba?" Noreen asked.

"I don't know. I don't see Communism as a threat to this country and I don't want my son to fight and kill Vietnamese people or be killed himself. Everything in me says it is wrong," said Elizabeth.

Denver said: "In my day, you fought for your country. You were willing to die for it. You didn't understand everything. You didn't question. You can't have every schoolboy determining foreign policy. You have to listen those who know what they're talkin' about."

"So old men send young men off to war? That's how it has always been. This is the generation that finally says 'No.' I think it's about time," Elizabeth said.

"Sally and Bryce can do anything," Denver said to Noreen as they drove to graduation, dressed in their cleaned-up best. "They have the smarts and enough money so they don't have to work. The scholarship made that possible for Sally. Why, they're heads-up sure of themselves."

Parking in a recently mowed field, Denver and Noreen walked across the stubble toward the bleachers, locating the rest of the family and joining them on the wooden planks. Graduates lined up in their caps and gowns. Benjy, who had recently received his draft notice, sat on one side of his mother, uncomfortable in a suit and tie. Bobbie's wife, Debbie, in a tight, short dress and spike heels, sat next to him. Next to Debbie, Elizabeth sat with her husband Daniel and fourteen-year-old Alice.

A few rows away, Denver noticed Sally's father, Benjamin, and a buxom young woman who clung to him as if he were something to hold on to. At least he had come—none of them had been certain that he would.

The day in late May was warm, but not summer-hot, not the searing 100 degrees that would soon embrace the valley. A slight wind carried the smell of an early harvested alfalfa crop.

The program began. Soon, the principal called on Sally, as valedictorian. Standing from the front row of graduates, she walked up the steps of the wooden platform, stepping deliberately in the unaccustomed high heels.

"To the graduating class of 1970," she began. "To our families and friends…"

Denver and Noreen watched proudly, grinning at each other, as if to say, "She's part of us." Since that day five years ago when they had taken peaches to the house with such far-reaching consequences, Noreen and Sally talked often on the telephone. Sally came to the farm whenever she could, simply falling in with whatever the older couple happened to be doing as if that was where she belonged.

She was fast friends with her cousin Bryce, a slight and earnest young man whom Bobbie and Benjy used to call "Sissy," because he played the trombone and was active in the school's Thespian Group. He was a rather good tennis player, his tall, thin frame agile and quick on the courts. When he became the number-one player, representing Kuna High School at the district and state level, he had earned begrudging respect from his cousins.

If Bryce knew that Sally was going to be at her grandparent's house, he would make an excuse to drop by. Denver treasured these visits by the two young people, listening as they talked, mostly about the war, which had become a raging inferno in both Vietnam and in America.

As Sally spoke, she stood tall and straight, her long, reddish-brown hair pulled back for the occasion so it fell behind her ears. Her face held a no-nonsense demeanor. She had shown them the dress she wore under the gown — honey-colored with a flared skirt, bought at Penney's with her mother's employee discount.

Denver wanted his parents and Emma to see Sally and Bryce, too. He wanted to say to them, "She has your hair. He has your eyes, your tone of voice," wanting to give each of them a part of today's joy, though most of the credit belonged to Sally.

"We, our generation, will question everything we have been taught, everything we learned from history. We will wrestle with the past, and with what is right. This generation—as none before it—dares to ask about the legitimacy of war, the right of old men to send young ones to foreign battlefields to die.

"My brother is in Vietnam. Every day I wonder if he will come home and what purpose his being there serves. Another brother has recently received his call to duty. This makes the issue a very personal one for me—for a number of reasons. Because I am female, I don't face the possibility of going to war for my country. Is that fair? I will soon be a college student. Just recently, protesting college students at Kent State were shot and killed merely for expressing their views on the war."

She paused and drank from the glass of water under the lectern.

"Women should have the right to choose what they do with their bodies and their lives. We will not be easy to live with. We, this generation, will shake every belief and reshape the world."

Her audience sat so still, almost as if they were not breathing. This day, this girl brought large matters in front of them, to Kuna, Idaho.

Perhaps she went too far. Denver felt some twinge of fear for her. Still war — and the world — had come so far in his lifetime: the trench-to-trench, hand-to-hand combat that his brothers knew in the First World War — "the war to end all wars"; the enormous toll, paid by young men like his son Harold, in the Second World War, and its dramatic ending with the explosion of the atomic bomb in Japan; the messy, uncertain Korean War; finally, now Vietnam with the blood dripping off the television set and into his living room every night.

Sally would stride forward, taking on every cause, asking every question, with the sureness of the young. He feared for her, though he would not stand in her path.

Everyone took pictures after the ceremony. Graduates hugged each other, cried and laughed, or stood awkwardly with their families, those people they had not wanted to recognize throughout high school.

"High school graduation is such a big thing," Noreen said to Denver. "Do you think they realize the life they've known is over?"

"Maybe they are starting to. Sally knows." They were walking through the crowd to their car, Alice between them, excited, dancing more than walking.

"Can you believe our Sally?" Alice said.

All those people heading toward their cars in the field of stubble kept stopping, seeing someone new, or waiting while a graduate tearfully hugged another.

"Will you take a picture for us?" a woman in a wide-brimmed hat and sunglasses asked Noreen, at the same time gesturing with her hand to the small cluster of people. "Move in closer! Charley, help your grandmother!"

"Denver Johnson. I'll declare! How long has it been!" a man asked. He was about Denver's age and walked with a serious limp. Denver recognized a neighbor who was often plowing his field across the road from where Denver worked his land. The two men exchanged pleasantries before moving on. In this manner, they slowly made their way to the car and home.

Before long, family members began arriving, greeting one another.

The buffet table was spread with delicious light cakes, potato salad, thin slices of roast beef rolled with horseradish inside, and a platter of crisp, colorful, raw vegetables.

A large glass bowl with matching cups was filled with punch. The cups were small and dainty with a loop handle that did not fit the men's hands, so they held on any way they could.

"Two swallows and it's gone," Denver smiled at Noreen.

Daniel, Elizabeth, and Bryce arrived in their fine blue luxury sedan, strolling across the lawn together, talking as they moved with slow and languorous movements, as if savoring the moment, the warmth of the day, letting this phase of Bryce's life drift away like light, white clouds. The three held hands, Elizabeth between the two men.

Emma started so much of this, but could not stick around for the finish, Denver thought. She would have been pleased with Noreen — perhaps she did not separate the bulbs as often as Emma would like, but she had taken the children to her bosom.

With each new arrival, hugs and kisses were exchanged and handshakes between the men.

Denver saw Sally pull up in her mother's car. Martha was in the passenger seat, Benjy and Debbie in the back. Benjy climbed out scowling, jammed his hands into his pockets, and slouched forward as he approached, alone, across the grass. Debbie got out and glanced around uncertainly. She stopped to light a cigarette. Martha and Sally got out and waited for Debbie, but she seemed reluctant to be with them.

"Benjy! Wait up!" She ran toward him, her shoes making her movements awkward. When she reached him, she held out the pack of cigarettes. He took one and smiled at her.

What will become of him? What will the military do to him? Denver wondered. Benjy had not excelled in school as Sally had. He was not as good-looking or athletic as Bobbie. He played the bully sometimes with younger kids or even with Sally. Other times, he lay on the couch at his mother's house, doing nothing except watching television, leaving empty milk glasses around and crumbs on sofa, floor, and table.

"Clean up after yourself!" Sally, who did most of the cleaning, had screamed at him one time when Denver and Noreen were there. "You're nothing but a bum!"

Sally and Martha arrived at the door about the same time as Benjy and Debbie. Buoyed by the attention Debbie paid him, Benjy lit into his sister as they entered.

"The nerve of you talkin' against the war when Bobbie is over there! Boy, if I go, I'll know where you're comin' from."

"I want the war to stop. I want Bobbie to come home, and you . . . even you, not to go."

"Even me? What's that supposed to mean?"

"Even bums like you...with nothing to do with their lives."

Denver cringed at Sally's derisive tone.

"Miss Know-it-All."

"Still, how is that not supporting you?"

As was often the case, Benjy had no answer. He stared back at her, blowing smoke into the air. This girl, this sister — her quickness had always bugged him. She outmaneuvered him playing Monopoly numerous times, whittling away at his real estate methodically. She would have Park Place and he would have Boardwalk, but two or three hours later, she would own both, with hotels, and he was marching toward defeat.

Debbie came to his rescue. "Aid and comfort, that's what my daddy says. He says you're givin' aid and comfort to the enemy by not supporting America." She tapped her foot and her arms were folded across her bosom, the cigarette dangling in her fingertips, the ash growing long.

Elizabeth moved quickly. "Hello, Debbie. Would you like an ashtray?"

"Hullo, Liz."

Benjy took the ashtray and held it for both of them.

"And what do you say?" Sally asked Debbie.

"Same as my daddy. Huh, Benjy?"

"Yep."

"Well, get back to me when you have a thought of your own," said Sally.

"You goin' to the drag races Saturday night?" Benjy asked his sister-in-law as conversation resumed among the guests.

It was natural enough for Benjy and Debbie to hang out together, with Bobbie gone. The high school crowd was dispersed so the ones who remained were frequently together. He was "safe" because of the family connection, but Denver wondered how safe he really was.

Bryce had been across the room when his cousins came in and had observed the conversation uneasily. A ripple of tension had passed through everyone. Denver did not want anyone to argue today. Still this war seemed to intrude itself into their lives like a plague.

About that time, Benjamin and his friend appeared at the door. Noreen went to greet them. Martha, at the opposite end of the room, engaged her brother-in-law, Daniel in a quiet and intense conversation. Both of them worked in the business community and were active in the Kuna Chamber of Commerce. Martha had gained Daniel's respect when they had worked together on a business development committee. Daniel had told Denver, "Clear to see where Sally got her brains. Martha is very bright, though she never saw herself as such. The store has been good for her — by representing Penney's in the business community she has grown."

Denver was glad for his older daughter. Indeed, as he looked at her now, she appeared well put together and confident, though he felt sure that her stance, with her back to the room so she didn't have to look at Benjamin, was no accident.

Benjamin surveyed the room, looked at the punch bowl and asked Denver, "Got anything stronger, Pops?" Some thickness in his tone indicated he'd probably had a few belts beforehand. He stood uncomfortably with his friend as she giggled nervously. Heavy make-up lined her face and ended at the jawline, creating an obtrusive line there.

Still, what a day! Denver smiled and hugged Sally and both his daughters, smiled again when Noreen looked in his direction. He sat in his large, comfortable recliner and talked with those who approached him. Of all the days and times he had had in this house, this was among the best.

Cameras clicked frequently as people ate and visited. Elizabeth orchestrated some photographs. "I want one of the graduates." She pulled Sally and Bryce together to stand in front of the mantel where a floral arrangement sat, with a sign saying "Congratulations" above it.

The inevitable time for taking Sally's family picture came. Elizabeth went over to her former brother-in-law. "If you'll excuse me just a moment. Benjamin, could I get a picture of Sally's family?"

"Be right back," Benjamin said, pulling his hand away from his friend.

"Hurry. I'll miss you." She smiled coyly, extending the hand that he had dropped as if it might be a string to pull him back. When he left her side, she looked around uncertainly. Noreen approached her.

"Come, get a plate. Have something to eat." Noreen led her toward the table. "Would you like to put your purse down?"

"No, no it's fine." She hiked it up to her shoulder.

"Well, if you aren't just the little spitfire!" Benjamin greeted his daughter. "Quite a speech you gave, young lady."

"Thank you for coming." Sally was uncertain as to how to respond, perhaps wanting his approval, still.

"Well, I can tell you, young lady, all you yellow-bellied Commie sympathizers don't deserve to live in this country. Your brother over there, and you sayin' things like that!" Benjamin's tone was harsh when he said this and louder than necessary.

Signaling Noreen to get everyone's attention, Denver said: "This is a day to be proud of Bryce and Sally. We'll have no more talk of war."

A brief silence followed; then Elizabeth said, "Come on, Benjy. We need you for this picture. And Debbie."

Sally stood in the middle of the picture, between her parents, who had finally nodded at each other and no more. Benjy stood next to his mother, while Debbie stood by her father-in-law. Just before the photo, Benjamin slid one arm around Sally and the other around Debbie. Everyone smiled.

The flash had not died before the five scattered. Sally held her mother's hand during the picture, though, and continued to hold it, while shrugging off her father's touch.

She spoke briefly with Debbie. Sally had removed her high-heeled shoes as soon as the ceremony was over. Debbie continued to wear her tall and tiny ones. Sally's hair was long and straight, while Debbie's was piled high on her head.

As soon as the cake was cut and presents opened, Benjamin said that he had to go.

"Thank you for coming." Sally held out her hand.

Benjamin ignored the hand, pulling her toward him in a bear-like embrace. "Did you mean to say thank you for coming, Father?"

Sally swallowed.

"What did you say, little girl?"

"Yes."

"Yes, what?"

Martha and Daniel began walking across the room toward the two.

"Yes, Father."

"I can't hear you."

"Yes, Father." She broke from him with a violent movement and ran outside.

"C'mon." Benjamin roughly pushed his woman-friend ahead of him out the door.

"Let's catch a ride with them," Benjy said to Debbie. "Wait a second, Dad. See you." The two were gone.

"Damn him! Today of all days! Why did he have to do that?" Martha said.

"He was looking for something from his daughter, and she was unwilling to give it," Noreen said, the abuse echoing in her from her own earlier experiences.

Bryce went outside after Sally, walking with her in the orchard. Shortly after, Alice went out, her light brown hair flying in the wind.

While Noreen, Elizabeth, and Martha cleared away dishes and cleaned up, Daniel and Denver watched the news, though Denver switched it off when the young people returned.

Sally was in good spirits again and her cousins were exuberant. They pulled out a game. "Who wants to play?"

As the light receded, everyone let go of earlier conflicts, talked quietly, and laughed often, now at ease.

"William's family will be here over the Fourth. We'd like to have a picnic in the orchard," said Noreen.

Elizabeth fell to planning with Noreen.

One early morning shortly after graduation, the telephone on the nightstand next to the bed rang, the noise slowly invading Denver's consciousness. Finally, he reached for the instrument.

Martha's voice came across, shaky and worn. "Bobbie's been hurt...he stepped on a land mine."

"Oh, no! How bad is it?"

"I don't know yet. They called Debbie."

"We'll come right over. Is Debbie there?"

"She's coming over."

"How did she sound?"

"Well, I didn't talk to her. Benjy phoned me."

"Benjy?"

"Yes, he was at her house when the call came. He's been there quite a bit lately."

"Staying there?"

"Well, he hasn't been here."

Several cars, including Benjamin's, were parked in the driveway of Martha's home when Denver and Noreen arrived. Sally opened the door.

Across the room, Martha sat in a large reclining chair, her hair disheveled, an old chenille bathrobe wrapped around her, at which she kept tugging and pulling as if it might protect her. On a small table next to her stood a black telephone. She didn't get up when the older couple approached but reached her arms toward them. They hugged.

A few feet away, Martha's ex-husband, Benjamin, sat in a worn plaid shirt and Levis, his arms folded across his body, quite still and alone, appearing somewhat dazed as if a boulder had struck him.

Denver noticed Benjamin's discomfort, how he stared straight ahead, not wanting to feel or notice the affection the others shared, perhaps, or to allow that he needed it. He couldn't cry. He was an unemotional man. He could fix cars. He could fuck women. He watched football. What else was there?

Denver went over and put out his hand. "Benjamin. I'm so sorry. I hope the injury…"

"It's bad. I just know it. Land mine accidents — that's when they lose parts of their body."

"Well, we don't know…"

"But we will."

When Noreen approached, she ignored the hand Benjamin extended, leaned over, and hugged him. "We're praying for Bobbie and for you, Benjamin." At this, Benjamin's thick black eyebrows knitted together quizzically as if he might ask: Why? I don't go to church. Praying didn't occur to me.

Denver had met Benjamin's parents only a few times, once when they sat stiff and unsmiling through a family dinner. The strictness of the Nazarene Church they attended, Denver thought, had the unintended result that people were either fully persuaded and led lives in harmony with the teachings, or simply left the church, as Benjamin had.

"Everything is a sin," Martha said once. "Going to the movies, dancing, roller skating, wearing a sleeveless dress or short skirt, even thinking bad thoughts. I think Benjamin gave up early leading that life. They believe in heaven and hell, but hell is what comes through loud and clear. I've never seen them joyful."

"Have you spoken with your parents?" Noreen asked Benjamin.

"No. I'll go over there later today. Doesn't do to upset their routine." The hug had dissipated his loneliness slightly. He seemed to reenter the room, come to his senses. Some part of him wanted to open, but seemed unable to find the key. He looked up at them. "Someone from the military…is supposed to be calling here soon…with more details."

Debbie sat at the kitchen table, wearing tight Levis torn at the knees and buttocks and a pink tank top without a bra, smoking continuously, an overflowing ashtray at her elbow. Across the table, Benjy sat sullenly staring into space. He too smoked nonstop. The pair did not look at each other or at anyone else. Their eyes met occasionally, but just as quickly glanced off.

When Debbie's parents came, Sally greeted them, leading them to their daughter. The three hugged. The parents looked around, not sure what to do next.

"Would you like to sit down?" Sally asked. "How about some coffee?"

Mr. Thompson, a short, stocky man with unruly brown hair and an intense manner, was the manager of a local freight company. He was accustomed to barking orders and giving directions. He spoke and moved in an abrupt, staccato manner. He wore a suit, tie, and a stiffly starched white shirt. Shorter than her husband, Mrs. Thompson appeared off balance, the mass of blonde hair swept high atop her head in a bouffant style, seeming to almost topple her.

Debbie's father stirred the coffee rather too long. Her mother made a couple of feeble attempts at conversation, finally looking down to stare at the cup she held.

No one knew what to do or how to be in this intimacy of pain. Everyday conversation didn't do, and words on the subject that had brought them together were weighed carefully and simply abandoned, as if none were adequate for this moment.

As the sun rose, Denver thought of all the mornings he had gone out to milk the cows, the frost crunching on the ground beneath his boots. How good it was to have a routine morning without pain or loss. His mother had died in the morning. All those mornings when Emma lay ill he hated waking, fearful that she would not wake, and then, one morning, she did not. Death often came in the early morning.

Sally was polite but distant toward her father, also afraid, perhaps, that he would blame her and her attitude about the war for her brother's injury.

The issue of Benjy and Debbie's relationship was out there too, the greater crisis putting the lesser one on hold.

Denver sat near the door, whether to flee or to prevent the entrance of anything else that might jar his family, he couldn't say. The cat walked across the living room, gaining the attention of Debbie's parents where they sat on the nubby green couch, and Benjamin, in a solid wooden chair. Benjy and Debbie watched from the kitchen, continuing to smoke absently, like breathing, automatically and numbly.

When the telephone rang, it jarred the air like broken glass. Martha picked it up. "Hello. Yes, yes, it is. Just a moment." She put her hand over the receiver and motioned to Debbie to pick up the telephone on the wall in the kitchen. The two women listened, and Denver thought he saw their worlds changing with the sounds coming from the instrument. Silence and dread spread across the room. Each person followed the murmured "uh-huh" from Martha, and then tears began running down her face.

Sally found a box of tissues, set it on the table by the telephone, and stood by her mother.

When the call ended, Martha pulled herself out of the chair, went to Debbie, and enfolded the younger woman in her arms. The others waited. Martha released Debbie, who stood dazed.

Sally went to her mother and held her, listening as her mother whispered and cried on her daughter's neck.

Sally absorbed the words quickly and turned to the others. "He's alive, but he has lost one leg, and an arm to the elbow, both on his right side. With severe loss of blood, they were afraid they might lose him, but they believe he will stabilize. They'll call with any change. When he improves enough, they'll fly him to Hawaii for further recuperation and they'll fly Debbie and Mom there to see him."

As the little group tried to absorb the news, their eyes turned to Debbie, whose hand shook now as she stubbed out her cigarette and did not light another one. Half-falling, she slumped onto a chair and gripped the table. "Oh, god."

"God damn Commies!" Benjamin stood up, his voice loud and angry. "Tearin' up my kid — Americans! I hope we bomb their asses back to the Stone Age!"

"As if that would help Bobbie!" Sally stood with her elbows out.

"Yeah, well if you damn Commie sympathizers hadn't been helping, they would have folded before this!"

"Yeah," Benjy said.

"You have the nerve to open your mouth! Sleeping with your brother's wife…" his mother whirled on him.

Debbie's parents' jaws fell open.

Mr. Thompson stood up from the couch where he and his wife had been sitting mostly in silence. He moved toward Benjy, his hands clenched, his face explosive like a soda can that has been shaken and is ready to burst.

Before he reached the younger man, however, Noreen spoke. "Our concern now is for Bobbie. I think we should pray together for him." She took Denver's

hand and extended her other one to Debbie's mother.
She began quietly humming, then singing as she
waited for the others to stand and hold hands.

>Amazing grace, how sweet the sound
>That saved a wretch like me.

At that moment, Elizabeth's family arrived. Denver offered his other hand to his daughter. Her family
fell in quickly, without question.

>I once was lost, but now am found
>Was blind, but now I see.

Benjamin turned, seeing the circle form. What to
do? He associated prayer more with guilt than solace.
Mr. Thompson had halted his progress toward Benjamin. Nearby, Martha stood ragged and broken.

>Through many dangers, toils, and snares,
>I have already come.

Benjamin wiped his hand against his side. Then he
reached it out to Martha, taking hers. She looked up
startled. He put his other hand out to Mr. Thompson.

>His grace has brought me safe thus far
>And grace will lead me home.

Martha reached for Benjy. His elbows rested on
the marbled Formica of the kitchen table. He held his

head in his hands. His mother laid her hand on his head. Sally put her hand over her mother's and took Debbie's hand with the other.

Finally, the circle completed, Noreen began to pray quietly, attempting to bring healing to the family, who had—for this moment at least—stopped shouting at each other. Denver wondered whether God or Noreen's belief held the balm.

When the prayer ended and the hands separated, there was an awkward silence. Then people began talking to each other.

Benjamin turned to Mr. Thompson and spoke quietly. The shorter man replied and gestured toward Benjy. Benjamin kept talking. By now, a normal color had returned to Mr. Thompson's face and he looked uncertain. Benjamin guided him back to where his wife stood, shook hands with both of them, and guided the couple to the door.

Denver watched in amazement.

"Thank you, Benjamin," Noreen said as Benjamin closed the door. "Thank you very much."

Benjamin took Noreen's hand. "Thank you." He shuffled his feet awkwardly.

For his part, when pressed, Benjy said he and Debbie were friends. They spent time together, talking and going out, but "we didn't do nothin' else."

Debbie said nothing. She had resumed smoking. "A fuckin' mess. I don't have nothin' to wear to Hawaii."

"Well, we'll help you, Debbie. You come down to the store where I work," Martha said.

"Oh, yeah, really? A bikini...do you think I could wear a bikini?" Debbie looked up half-brightly, as if she had found a reason for going.

"We'll see what there is." Martha turned to Elizabeth, who had by now been told about Bobbie's condition. Elizabeth put her arm around her sister and led her to the bedroom.

"Benjy." The father approached his son. "I don't want you to set foot in Debbie's house. Is that clear? You do and you're out of a job."

The job held little consequence for him, since he would soon be leaving to serve in the military. "We didn't do nothing."

"You mean you didn't do anything?" Sally said.

"You're not my goddamn teacher! D-dum..." starting to refer to her as he and his brother had in the past, but as he looked around, he saw Daniel, Bryce, and his grandfather, perhaps saw himself as these others would. The words died on his tongue.

"Sally, help your mother by making phone calls and doing shopping for her. And, help Debbie. Maybe you should go with her to Hawaii?" said Benjamin.

Startled, Sally looked up at her father in disbelief, finally saying, "Okay. Yes, Father." Then she reached out to him and hugged him. Benjamin's eyes glistened and the muscles along his jaw and in his arms seemed to loosen.

"Go to your brother," Benjamin said gently.

Sally turned and walked toward Benjy, who had resumed smoking, looking sullen and passive. She moved toward him hesitantly. He was still seated at the table. She put her arm on his shoulder. "How you doin' bro?"

Conflicting emotions crossed Benjy's face: a momentary softening of muscle, then a tensing again, as if in blood and bone he was searching for his own reaction. The gentler direction lost. It took the boy too deep, Denver thought, spilling him into some dark emotional pool that was black and impenetrable and seemed to have no bottom or edges, so he quickly returned to the surface. He shrugged, dismissing Sally's touch, concentrated on inhaling deeply and blowing a smoke ring into the air.

He seemed younger than his years and, at the same time, aged, lacking freshness or purpose.

Later, on the way home, Denver said, "That Benjy — I don't know what's to become of him."

"Yes, he's quite unreachable."

"And Debbie — the way she was dressed. I don't know what these young people are coming to."

"Maybe they will mature, but right now...I could smell liquor on both of them."

"We would never have embarrassed our parents or ourselves in the community like that."

"All that has changed though, hasn't it? Benjy might be embarrassed at having been caught, but I don't think by what he did. But, outside of a circle of acquaintances — who knows or cares? Who pays any attention — except as something to gossip about?" Noreen commented.

"Yep. A lot has changed, not necessarily for the better," Denver added.

Noreen continued, thinking about various family members: "Some—like Sally or Elizabeth's kids, probably William's kids, will be fine, but except for Sally the others have strong families. Elizabeth and Daniel go to church. I don't know about William and Susan. I don't think Martha and Benjamin ever went very much."

Denver replied, "I suppose Emma and I could have been a better example. As the kids got older, we were busy on the farm, and we didn't go to church so much. We started going when Harold joined the army. I remember Emma saying that she was praying for Harold, but she thought there were others more worthy praying, and she reckoned that God understood German. How could he answer all those prayers?"

"I don't know the mind of God, but the act of praying prepares us for whatever the results are." Noreen said.

"So you don't know whether, say one-hundred people of faith are praying for one soldier, it makes him any safer?"

"No, I don't. I only know that when I talk to God, it helps me."

"Yes, and me. You know, I like saying Harold's name and Emma's. I like hearing those sounds. It continues them in some way. Do you believe they are with God?"

"Yes. Do you?" Noreen asked.

"I hope so."

Though it was the height of the season on the farm, Denver and Noreen spent much of the next few days at Martha's home.

Denver had called William. Ronald, the grandson who was to come ahead of the rest of the family, would not. The family would drive up together.

"Ronald will be disappointed," William said, "but clearly it isn't the right time. You have your hands full with the farm and Martha. I'll call her. How's Debbie holding up?"

"Okay, I guess. She's staying with her parents for a while. She gave up the apartment. I guess she'll be going to Hawaii to see Bobbie."

Both Benjy and Debbie continued to deny that their relationship was anything other than friendship. Benjy stayed at his mother's house, skulking in and out, not wanting his mother's attention.

"Mom's having a really hard time with this," Sally said to Noreen and Denver. They had stopped in to check on everyone. "She wants to see Bobbie, but she's not thrilled about going with Debbie."

"At least she doesn't have to worry about you." Noreen said.

Martha came out of her bedroom and joined the conversation.

"The boys need me, especially Bobbie now," Martha said. "Goodness knows when or if he will ever be able to be on his own."

A skittering of fear ran through Denver's gut, slight but gnawing.

"It may seem like that right now—he and you took a really tough blow, but life will go on. The army will fit Bobbie with really fine artificial limbs. He will be able to do things, in time."

Denver thought his daughter didn't hear him. "Bobbie will have to have care and I don't think he's going to get it from Debbie. I'll take care of him. And there's Benjy. I've told him Bobbie is never to know anything about his relationship with Debbie—whatever it was. He's probably using drugs and has no ambition. He does whatever is easy. Why does Sally have so much drive and Benjy doesn't have any push to do something with his life?"

"Seems like the boys followed their father...which is normal...and he wasn't a very good leader. Though he's stepped up to the plate in this crisis."

"Yes, he has. A little late, wouldn't you say?"

When they heard the car stop, Denver looked out the window. He saw William pulling himself out of the driver's seat, leaning slightly against the door, looking, as if this scene—the land, the trees, the house, the old barn, and the mountains beyond—were a cold drink he'd been needing. Absently, William moved his tall, broad body away from the car and closed the door softly, as if not to disturb his thoughts—the ghosts and the memories that were spread before him in the hot July day.

In California, in his corporate and suburban world with his family, William's past would be pushed to the back of his mind, hidden in an area of "yesterday," because none of it was a pressing demand. Here, the container opened, briefly obliterating that Golden State. His mind, under that head of light brown hair, was filled with all that had taken place here.

His wife, Susan, blonde hair long and loose, and the children, Sarah and Ronald, walked toward the house. William shoved his hands into his pockets and moved slowly. He would have told his family, on the way, to fill the long miles of the Nevada desert—this happened here, and I remember, and one time—and they would have indulged him, even asking questions sometimes, if sufficiently bored and nothing else was going on. The kids would have grown restless with the games brought along. William was anticipating, and the rest of them caught a glimpse.

Now Denver watched his son, in an open-collared green golfing shirt—reveling in memory, taking it slow. Perhaps it loomed greater to him than to Elizabeth or Martha, who had always lived in this area, not separated from it by another life, another place.

Twelve-year-old Sarah turned and ran to her father, saying something to him. He pointed toward the barn. Taking her hand, the two strolled through the grass together. She was slender and gawky, with freckles, her grandmother's thick reddish-brown hair and something else—was it the cut of her chin and nose that brought Emma and a twinge of pain to Denver's mind?

Ronald hopped restlessly around his mother, waiting for the other two. "Come on, you guys." At ten, he was blonde and restless, in a T-shirt and cutoffs. No doubt it would keep them all busy trying to keep that one occupied. This trip down memory lane wouldn't have been his choice, but his parents wanted him to know their Idaho family. Susan's parents lived two hours away from them in Southern California. The boy would endure it all patiently, indulging his parents. Years later, when someone said "Idaho" on the news or in conversation, he would start and listen.

Then the door was open. The greetings and hugs began, and everyone asking, "How was the trip?" Though William's family had been invited to stay at Elizabeth's, they chose to stay on the farm instead with Denver and Noreen. Ronald and William brought the bags in, and Noreen and Susan got the family settled upstairs.

By now the summer's heat had arrived with the long, languid evenings when the light stayed until ten o'clock. The children exulted in the relaxation of bedtime hours.

"Can we sleep outside? Can we have Alice over?" Sarah and Ronald asked a day or so after they arrived. Susan and Noreen agreed, and the three children spent much of the afternoon and evening running barefoot in and out of the house, building their nest for the night. A flashlight, a game, a pillow, something to eat—all were important to the excursion.

While the children had fun, the adults visited. They talked over Bobbie's plight, and the war that had hit them at home. They felt the burden of the situation, but also — and perhaps because of — Bobbie's injuries, they wanted this vacation to be carefree for the children.

The next day, the kids wanted to go to the canal. William, fearful of the children going by themselves, but still wanting them to experience one of the pleasures of his youth, went with them. The children were good swimmers, but the two from California were used to swimming pools with known depths and edges.

Susan joined them. The five set out along a dusty trail wearing swimsuits, with a picnic basket and beach towels thrown over their shoulders.

"Wait for us." Turning, the group saw Sally and Bryce running to catch up with them. Behind them came their grandfather, lean and brown, not looking sixty-two, smiling, wearing a pair of cut-offs that Noreen had found.

William stuck out his arm, raising it slowly in an arch above his head, an inclusive, welcoming gesture. "Where's Noreen?" He asked when the others approached.

"She wanted to read and nap. I have some irrigating to do, but it can wait."

"I'll do it with you, Dad."

"We've worn Noreen out," Susan said.

"No — certainly it is more activity than we're used to, but Noreen loves having you here. Better to wear out than rust out."

Sally and Bryce caught up with the younger kids and all of them talked and laughed excitedly as they walked.

When they reached the canal, the children dropped whatever they carried and jumped in the water.

Susan unfolded the chair she was holding. "Will, are you sure the kids are safe? Are there any rocks they might hit?"

"They're okay. The kids have been coming to this hole since William was a boy," Denver assured his daughter-in-law.

The afternoon was long and languid, the adults dozing, chatting, reading, or taking care of feeding the children or lathering them in sunscreen when they ran up dripping and excited.

"Hurry, Momma." Sarah's feet danced. "I have to get back in."

"This is the life." William leaned back, arms extended behind his head. "Welcome to Idaho. Turn your clocks back twenty-five years, or so says a bumper sticker we saw."

"Funny. Do you know this is the first time I've ever come to this spot?" Denver said. "I was too busy — or thought I was — when you kids were growing up. And the grandkids, well, I still thought I had to be working every moment. I should have taken a few afternoons off to come here — with Harold and

Bobbie and especially Benjy. Can't say what difference it would have made, but it wouldn't have hurt."

"Yeah, that's a tough one." William's eyes were
shut. He squinted occasionally in the direction of the
children. He seemed unwilling to take up any serious
matter, as if he were memorizing this quiet afternoon,
this comfortable family group, this land, to have with
him, somewhere inside, so he could retreat when the
business meetings became interminable and the demands for profit, profit, and more profit came at him
like arrows.

"It's so good to have you here." Denver said.

By early evening, they gathered up drink containers, towels, and everything else they'd brought and
went back to the house, where Noreen had prepared a
dinner of meat loaf, corn on the cob, salad, hot bread,
and watermelon.

"It's the long evenings that I remember so much.
That feeling of freedom because there's no school and
maybe summer will go on forever," said William.

After dinner, William walked to the field of seed
corn with his father and son, Ronald, following along.

"I swear that corn grew a foot since yesterday."
William said.

Each man carried a shovel and, upon reaching the
field, they began moving dirt to change the path of
the water and irrigate new rows. Ronald found a stick
and made trails with the water and dirt.

"Seems like it. It's very satisfying, watching crops
grow. I've done it all my life, but it took—I guess it

took your mother and Noreen and time—for me to appreciate this life."

"It seems so simple to me now, so natural and direct. My work…is so different." William paused to gaze across the field, as if he could never look at it enough. "Indirect, I guess is how I would describe what I do. Say I make a proposal—how to handle claims more efficiently. Any change is unnerving to the company, so you have to stick your neck out, explain, justify, and document. Then everyone has to talk about it, defend their territory, and worry about what their place would be in any new configuration. Meetings are held at every level. Changes are made in the original proposal. There's so much talk, and power and personalities go into it, and so much lag time before change is made or results seen, it's hard to recognize what you started with and even harder to measure whether it actually worked."

"I see what you mean, but it pays well. My generation never thought about job satisfaction. The pleasure was in having a roof over our head and food on the table," Denver responded.

"Yes, I suppose that's true, Dad. Our lives are a good deal more comfortable. Still, that hinges on the paycheck. The house is in an area that's safe and the schools are good—and we have college yet to come."

"College. Just to go to school at all was such a privilege. I went more than some of the older kids. That's all changed now, of course."

"Yes, and I'm not complaining, just explaining, I guess. Susan plays tennis at the country club and is active in all the kids' activities. My job makes a good life for the family."

"You play some golf, I guess."

"Yes. Not as much as I'd like. Usually it's connected with business."

"I'm proud of you son. You've done very well."

"Thanks. Susan tells me that and I hear it at work. Only thing is…it isn't as satisfying as it once was. Oh, well… When will you harvest this field?"

"If it stays hot, I'd guess late August, or first week in September. Seed corn pays a lot better than corn for eating, you know. Noreen figured that all out."

"Did she? She's a fine woman. You feeling good, Dad?"

"Yes, I am. A twinge of arthritis once in a while, but doc says I'm healthy as a horse." The men had stopped and were leaning on their shovels for the moment. Denver noticed Ronald playing in the dirt, making small ditches, directing small amounts of water to go in a new direction. He had almost forgotten the child was there.

"It's this life. Staying close to nature…knowing who you are." William said.

"What do you mean? Sounds like something they'd say in California."

"Yes, I suppose, but you've never measured yourself against another," William commented.

"Oh, you're wrong there, son. You see another farmer with better fences, healthier looking crops, a nicer house or barn; it's easy to compare. When your mother died, I felt like a failure…didn't think I could

make a go of the farm and knew I couldn't do anything else. I got another chance."

"I didn't know that's how you felt. I know I didn't
come around much when Mom died. I'm sorry for
that. Seems like it takes half your life to figure out
what's important."

"At least half. But this young man, now he'll pick
it up much quicker than I did." Denver smiled toward
Ronald.

"I want him to remember this, and to know who
he is."

"I'm Ronald." The boy came to his father's side,
grinned up at him and took his hand. "That's who I
am. Won't I always be Ronald?"

"Yes, you will," William smiled down at the boy.
Looking on, Denver liked seeing the comfortable
warmth between the two, also realizing he'd never
been that way when his children were growing up.

The evening grew late as the three made their way
to the house, ambling, stopping here and there to
check the fruit in the orchard and to pick some cherries, eating and spitting the seeds on the ground.

Ronald listened as his father and grandfather
talked. The young boy did not urge them back to the
house; rather he seemed to be absorbing their words
and his surroundings, or just relaxing, because it was
easy to do that here.

When they reached the house, Ronald went inside,
joining his sister and the rest of the family. William
and Denver sat on the step. It was nearly dark. Frogs

croaked from a ditch bank nearby. Crickets sang. The air was still and shirtsleeve warm.

"It cools off much quicker in the evenings where we live. These long evenings are…I don't know…like a bonus at the end of the day."

"I was wonderin'…are you happy with your life, son?"

"Huh…no reason not to be. Susan's a good wife and mother. The kids are fine. We live a comfortable life."

The two sat silent for a while.

"I don't know if I can do this forever though… pushing myself to go to work to get a paycheck." William said.

"Everyone feels like that sometimes. You could do something else."

"Yes, but what? If I quit my job tomorrow, I'd have to look for another one, and to get the same pay it would be a similar job. What would I gain? Seems like…you set your course for life when you're still wet behind the ears. When I was in high school, parents were so proud if their kid went to college. Brains over brawn, you know. White collar better than blue. I'm not saying I regret any of it, but you start climbing the corporate ladder, sometimes you look up ahead, tryin' to figure out what the reward is for getting farther up. Money and prestige, of course…"

"I wish my dad could hear you talk, speakin' as if money weren't enough. Money and what it buys. You know, son, you come back here in the summer for a few days and bask in the rural life and start talkin'

like this. Don't you forget — to have that corn growing, and the fruit ripening, and all, we work sun up to
sun down, six days a week, at least seven months of
the year. Most of the years, I milked cows through the
winter months. There's no security, no pension plan.
You see, son, you and your generation — you've never
been hungry."

"You're right, Dad, and because I've never been
hungry, survival has never been an issue. Job and life
satisfaction has."

The two men were silent again, each enveloped in
his own light and darkness.

"It's so good for our kids to come up here and just
sort of naturally be a part of everything," Susan said
one evening. She was from California, and somewhat
more casual than Denver was used to. The kids ate
anywhere and most any time. If not otherwise occupied, they watched television.

"I must be getting old. It's not the way I was
raised." Denver made these observations to Noreen as
they were getting ready for bed one night.

"No. Not you. They're okay. They do what I ask.
When they have a snack, they take care of the dishes
and pick up after themselves. They aren't rude or
mean."

"As usual, you've helped me put things in per-
spective." Denver turned out the light and drew her
to him, taking comfort and warmth from her body.
He drifted into sleep holding her lightly.

They left the windows open at night, the cool air
floating in and around like a blessing. In the early

light of morning, bird songs flew among the sleepers. The adults heard the notes in varying degrees while the children, deeper in sleep, heard nothing.

And then it was the Fourth of July, 1970—a day for a picnic. Everyone was coming except Debbie, and that to the relief of the rest of the family.

Noreen, Elizabeth, and Susan planned the food, giving Martha an easy assignment—potato chips, carrot and celery sticks. Young Sarah found the croquet set and the badminton net.

William dug around in a shed and found the hand-crank ice cream freezer. Noreen pulled out the recipe. The sweet, milky liquid was soon poured into the round metal container and placed inside a wooden bucket. Ice and salt were put around the can. Then the churning began.

"I get to be first!" Ronald turned the handle, but soon wearied. Sarah, Alice, then Sally, and Bryce stopped by from the other preparations they were making to take their turns.

"Keep it turning," their grandfather admonished as each round grew harder and it became a game as to who could turn it at all.

William put a feedbag over the top. "Sit on it," William said to Ronald, continuing to turn the handle. When he could turn it no longer, he declared, "It's done," and Noreen came out on the porch, wiping her hands on her apron.

"We'll need to pack it, but first we have to pull the dasher."

"You don't want to miss this," William said to Ronald. "Where did Sarah go? Sarah!"

Soon Sarah came from the direction of the orchard where she had been helping set up sawhorses and long plywood sheets to form tables. Sally and Bryce came, along with Alice.

Noreen carried out a long plate, a big spoon, and several smaller ones. William took the top off the ice cream, and quickly, so it wouldn't melt, Noreen began pulling the dasher out, pushing the ice cream that stuck to it back into the container.

"Leave some for tasting!" the kids squealed, and she left rather more than she might have. She set the dasher on the long plate and spoons came from everywhere to get a cool, sweet taste before it melted. Then, to the satisfied smack of lips, Noreen and William closed the container, added ice in the wooden bucket, poured coarse salt generously around the outside, and put feedbags over the top.

William and Denver carried the frozen prize a few feet to the fruit cellar, bending their heads as they entered the low stone building built into the ground, where it was cooler than anywhere else.

In there, the air was dank and heavy. Cobwebs covered the two small windows. A light bulb in the ceiling at the center of the room was inadequate, so the corners receded into a feathery darkness.

"This place always seemed mysterious to me as a kid." William looked around at shelves that contained a few jars of canned fruit.

"We don't can much anymore, with just the two of us."

"Do you know what I mean about the place?" William asked.

"Yes, I think I do, though I guess it's just a feeling."

"It's the kind of place they use in the movies for the dark things to happen."

"Yes, it feels a little ghostly to me. There are the jars that my mother, and then Emma, used. Their fingerprints might still be on some of them...and they, themselves, so long gone."

By midafternoon, lawn and folding chairs had been carried to the orchard. Twelve-year-old Sarah turned in great earnestness to setting up the croquet game. She borrowed a tape measure from her grandfather and placed the wire wickets apart evenly throughout the lawn.

Martha arrived. Benjy drove in his own car, the low-rider bumping along the lane, making loud guttural varooming noises. Everyone looked up.

Clipboard in hand, Sarah asked everyone, "Do you want to be in the tournament?" She persisted in organizing her event, frustrated but not quitting when others were offhanded about it.

"That young woman's gonna take over the world one of these days," her father mused.

"Benjy," she called when he arrived and stood leaning on his car, smoking, a cool observer on the scene, "Will you play in the croquet tournament?" She ran toward him, barefoot through the grass.

The two talked briefly. He crushed his cigarette beneath his shoe in the gravel and followed her.

Carried along by Sarah's enthusiasm everyone agreed to play, though Elizabeth and Susan dropped out quickly, chatting and moving between yard and kitchen, where preparations continued. Denver, William, and Daniel visited on the edge of the game, between turns, interrupted often by calls to fetch this or that.

The whack of wooden mallet against ball came clean, certain, and regular.

"I hit you!" Ronald insisted when his ball rolled next to Benjy's ball.

"No, you didn't."

"A touch is a hit." This from the imperious Sarah, her bare feet jumping around, excited. She objectively administered the rules and everyone obeyed her, indulging her at first, but gradually coming to respect her rulings.

"She plays at home," Susan commented while working with Noreen and Elizabeth in the kitchen. Noreen iced a lemon cake with rich butter icing.

"It shows. She's good. I didn't know kids still played that game."

"William bought the kids a set a couple of years ago."

"Well, she's quite an organizer."

When Benjy hit Sally's ball and, putting his foot on his own, whacked his sister's across the lawn, far from where she had been, he grinned in great pleasure. "So there, smarty pants!"

Sally grimaced, but said nothing.

"Whoa!" Bryce said. "What a hit!"

Denver noted Benjy's pleasure, something the young man didn't allow himself to show often. His triumphs over his sister had been few.

The sun beat hot and clear, insects buzzed, the mallets cracked, and bare feet bounced in the grass. Denver's world would have been perfect, had it not been for the image of Bobbie, lying somewhere, horribly mutilated, and that for life.

He thought of the tall, athletic, rather handsome young man with high cheekbones and symmetrical features. What would Bobbie be when they saw him again? Before he left, he was often unshaven, his hair dirty and uncombed, his clothes worn until they were ratty. That look was popular and didn't seem to bother the young women that Bobbie knew.

"The army will take care of that," Denver had said.

When he came home after boot camp, his bare head looked strangely vulnerable and less protected above the uniform. He stood taller and straighter— the army did that, too.

Bobbie's eyes had changed over the years, going from the wonderment they held when he was a small boy to the world-weary, jaded look of a teenager. The flash and excitement left, whether for good or temporarily Denver couldn't guess.

Saying goodbye to Bobbie, Denver had shaken the young boy's hand. "We'll be thinkin' about you...and

prayin'…Noreen's better at that than I am." He had
pulled the young man to him in a rough embrace.

Bobbie had looked at his grandfather with attention, the dullness gone momentarily from his eyes.
Cutting away from the easy dismissal the young often
make of their elders, Bobbie seemed as if he wanted
to memorize his grandfather. The tractor rides. The
time they had fished the Wood River. As if he suddenly saw his youth gone and wondered why he had
wanted it to happen.

Now Denver looked down at the stub of a finger
on his right hand and thought it was nothing. The
pain was a settled and distant memory.

He hoped that Bobbie's dissolution was temporary, and Benjy's, too. He tried to catch the young
man's dark eyes with his own.

Benjy's eyes were elusive, though, and half-closed.
Benjy of the ragged and grubby clothes, dirty fingernails and greasy brown ponytail, the ever-present
dangling cigarette and sullen face, playing croquet
with little Sarah, teasing her and her standing up to it,
not wavering.

"Go get 'em," Sally called encouragement to Sarah.

How could Sally come from this family — almost
he said "of losers" — to himself and then denied it. She
was not beautiful, no, her brother's faces were perhaps better sculpted, hers longer and thinner, but you
forgot because her brown eyes burned with intensity
and passion to know the world and do something

about its flaws. Purpose burned in her, along the slender browned arms and body.

Martha had gained weight in the last few weeks after the news had come about Bobbie. With her brooding acceptance that trouble followed her like a faithful dog, she took disaster as her natural-born companion.

The croquet match — interrupted innumerable times and held together only by Sarah's will — came to a final between Benjy and Sarah. Benjy had physical strength, while Sarah was deadly accurate and had a cunning knowledge of the game that escaped her cousin.

Her red ball hid behind a wicket from Benjy's yellow one. He hit too hard, his game suffering from his overzealous approach.

Everyone had to see the final. Sarah commanded it. In cotton shorts and a light blouse, Noreen came out of the kitchen to watch, along with Elizabeth, Martha, and Susan. William, Denver, and Daniel stood in the shade so the women could sit in the lawn chairs.

Sally, Bryce, Ronald, and Alice cheered each clever move or tricky shot. Sally got the camera.

"You're runnin' scared," Benjy mumbled to Sarah. "Runnin' scared." He kept it up until he unnerved her briefly so she hit badly, leaving her ball in the open. Then he hit it, and then placed his shoe on his ball and knocked hers away in the opposite direction. Then he put his own through the finish and raised his mallet into the air.

"Winner! Winner, here!" Benjy crowed. Everyone clapped.

"Time to eat. We need everyone to help carry things," Noreen said.

Inside, Noreen lifted Tupperware containers filled with potato salad, deviled eggs, and Jell-O molds in bright colors from the refrigerator, placed them in ready hands, and pulled out the huge half-moon wooden bowl of green salad. Loaves of bread, warmed in aluminum foil, emerged from the oven and were placed in baskets, along with baked beans in a large earthenware pot with a heavy handle.

"Be careful with it," Susan admonished, handing the pot to Benjy.

Near the orchard, William and Daniel tended the barbecue, turning the chicken pieces and brushing them with a dark brown sauce, broiling hamburgers and hot dogs, as well, talking as they worked. Both had growing families and financial responsibilities; both were in business.

"So, we're on for golf tomorrow?" Daniel asked William.

"Yes. What time do we tee off?"

"Seven o'clock. Is that too early?"

"No. I like early mornings."

When all the food was out, Noreen came to the orchard and checked the table. The young ones had paper plates and were eyeing the food greedily, held off by their mothers, waiting for Noreen's signal.

"Let's hold hands and pray," she said. They did. Denver held Noreen's hand. For that moment, the cares and concerns of their lives receded slightly. They were a family, here on this land where they had worked, lived, died, argued, commiserated, made love, and grown throughout the century.

Everyone filled a plate and sat down at the red-and-white clothed tables, under the peach, plum, and apple trees.

"So Sally, once you get to Stanford you're more than halfway to our house. You come down and see us every chance you get."

"Sure, I will. Guess I'll be pretty busy at first..."

"I'm sure you will, but you'll adjust. I get up there on business, too, so..."

"So, a good reason for me to go with you," Susan said, "My folks are usually willing to come and stay with the kids for a day or so."

"She'll probably be busy protestin'." Benjy munched his food, "while I'm fightin.'"

No one responded immediately. Alice, Sarah, and Ronald kept on chattering in their circle, a little apart from the others. A couple of other conversations continued, but began trailing off, as if the life had been sucked away. Benjy's comment captured everyone's attention.

The air seemed hotter and stiller, the insect buzz louder. In the distance, they heard the noise of a chain saw.

"Who would be working today?" Susan asked.

"Farmers. The work is never done." Noreen swiped at a fly near her plate.

Martha, sitting in a lawn chair, looked down at her plate. She wore a long, straight, flowered dress, comfortable and nonbinding. With her fork, she poked and stirred the brown beans on her plate. "This war is tearing us all up."

"Yes, it is. We all feel so bad about Bobbie," Sally said.

"Then how can you protest?" Denver was surprised at his own words. It was in the air, this war, their Bobbie, too big and broad to confront and too close at hand to ignore. Until now, Denver had said little except to Noreen, but now he did. "I don't see how you can have people in the street making foreign policy. I've never seen the like. My brothers fought in the first war. Harold died in the second one. They never asked if the war was right. You defend your country."

Sally put down her plate and came close to her grandfather, listening, absently brushing long strands of hair from her intent face.

"I know, Granddad. I know how you feel, but this war is different. Our country isn't threatened. The goals are obscure."

"Except if you understand communism's intent to take over the world." Denver said. "You look at a map. See how much of the world communism dominates now. They got Eastern Europe after the Second World War. China is communist. The Soviet Union... is a real threat."

"So we destroy the people of Vietnam and the country because of that threat. The end justifies the means—I don't think so," Elizabeth said.

"Cowards, those guys who won't go." Benjy looked to where Bryce sat among the tall wild grasses.

"You may have to go," Noreen said to Bryce. "Do you worry about it?"

"I just turned eighteen. I don't know. I don't support the war—sorry, granddad, I respect your view. It comes from experience and the past and makes perfect sense, but Vietnam is not a threat to our country and, like Mom said, I don't think the end justifies the means." The young man spoke slowly and clearly, without emotion, as if he were learning what he thought just ahead of saying it.

He had lived to some extent in the family shadows—slender and wiry, he was less physical than Bobbie and Benjy, and though he had done well in school, he hadn't excelled as had Sally. He wasn't forceful in his presence or opinions, nor argumentative, nor inclined to dominate. He came out to help his grandparents occasionally, irrigating or planting, weeding, or working in the orchard, thinning out the peaches, doing whatever was needed. He and his grandfather had often worked together, without conversation, for long periods, in a companionable silence.

"He's easy to be around," Denver had told Noreen. To Bryce, "You were sure a lot of help today. I really appreciate you comin' out."

"No problem, Granddad. I like helping."

"What are you reading now?" Noreen asked.

"Dostoyevsky — some of his shorter work." Bryce smiled, a slow easy smile creasing his face naturally as if it were used to smiling. He was not compelled like Sally, and was somewhat easier to have around — less intense, more at home with himself.

Benjy leaned toward Bryce. "You wouldn't run to Canada…"

"I don't know."

"If Bryce doesn't believe in the war and if he gets called up, I'm telling you," Elizabeth spoke calmly, "I would lie, cheat, or steal to keep him out of it."

"A war fought in the media," Daniel added. "What a horrible blow for Bobbie."

"Yes." Martha looked down, old and tired.

"You'll be going to see him soon in Hawaii." Noreen turned to Martha as she said it.

"Yes. I have to. Debbie doesn't want me to, I know, but…I'm not sure how much she cares about him."

"Bobbie will come home to my house. I'll take care of him." Martha crossed her arms and sat back a little in her chair. "Somebody's gotta do it. Is that what you think I should have done, Elizabeth — lied or cheated to get Bobbie out, or keep Benjy away?"

Benjy scowled, lit a cigarette, and looked away. He had not questioned going into the military when he was called.

"No. It's a personal issue and, even with Bryce, if he believed in the war and felt he should go, I'd support him, though I don't agree with it."

"He's not likely to believe in it living around you," Benjy said.

"He has a mind of his own. Denver's point is a different one, though. Everyone can't make foreign policy. Everyone can't decide for themselves whether they will go to war or not," Noreen said.

"True, but if the people don't believe in the war, as has happened in this one, there will be increasing resistance to sending more young men." Sally glanced over the assembled family members. "You know… World War I was supposed to be the war to end all wars, well…this one will come closer to being that because of the media coverage and because the young people who are likely to go have said 'why,' and 'what for,' and 'no more war,' and they are having an impact."

A brief silence ensued, as if the war had worn them all out. Martha sat disconsolate.

Elizabeth saw her troubled sister and needed to help her. "All this is beside the point when it comes to Bobbie. We love him and will do whatever we can to help and support him when he comes back."

"He will live with the consequences of this war for the rest of his life," Martha said. "And the fact that it is an unpopular war will affect him. He doesn't come home to a hero's welcome or the warm response of grateful people."

"You're right, mother. The price of this war will go on for a long time. He isn't dead though, that is something to be thankful for," Sally said.

"Yes, but there may be times when he'll wish he was," Martha commented quietly.

Slowly, then, they turned away from the war. Sarah and Ronald, sitting barefoot in the grass, grew restless with the talk and wanted to know, "When can we have ice cream?"

"I think about now," William answered. "Okay if I get it, Noreen?"

"Sure. Maybe we should carry some of this food back."

The sun was low over the Owyhee Mountains when the bowls were heaped with rich vanilla ice cream. The air was warm and moving slightly, carrying the scent of onion and alfalfa. Mosquitoes grew active. Susan handed around insect repellent.

The ripening fruit hung above them, green globes in the evening shadows. All around, the fertile world buzzed, grew large under the ground or into the sky, changed shape, color, and size, a kind of restless activity taking place all around them. The valley of farmland stretched before them in the long evening.

Denver did not want it to end—he would have them all stay in this moment. William would be taking his family and returning to California and a corporate career of which he had grown weary. Benjy would go to war, and Bryce might, also.

"It gets dark too early in California," William said.

"It's so different here," Susan said. "Time seems suspended. The neighbors distant. I don't know that I could live here, but to visit, it's great."

Hearing his mother, Ronald came to her. "I could live here. I want to be a farmer when I grow up, like Granddad."

"Why? It's a lot of hard work for not much money. Isn't that true, Denver?"

"Well, yes, sometimes. Other times you do all right. But, there are no guarantees."

"But it's free…you don't have any boss."

"You're slave to wind and weather. To water and insects and soil. To sick animals and to the market. Tell you what…you come up and spend a summer. Not on vacation, just workin' here with us. You'll have a better idea if you want to do it for a lifetime."

"Oh, goody. Can I, Momma?"

"Well, we'll have to talk to your father…"

"Son," Denver said later to William when the others were not around. "If the job gets to be too much, you could come back and farm. I could gradually retire and you could take over."

William's blue eyes lit up. "Thanks, Dad. I'll remember that…even if I never do it." From the sound of his voice trailing off, Denver supposed that his son knew it would never happen. Susan would not want to leave California. The children were in school there. There was not enough money in the farm, but it would be there, to pass through his mind when the corporate world grew tedious.

They had carried everything out of the orchard, and then sat in the yard in the still warm air as the last light of the sun left, hearing firecrackers in the distance. Sarah, Ronald, and Alice had sparklers and lit the dark with the tiny spots of brilliance. The children wanted to sleep out that night, again, to hold onto the day as long as possible.

Denver thought that it sunk into each of them — this peaceful day, this unit of belonging — because of Bobbie and the war that raged on, and because of Benjy and Bryce and the uncertain future. Even Benjy had not left early. He had scowled. He had growled. He had taunted Sarah, but he had stayed.

Chapter Eight

In early August, when the corn stood well over
Denver's head, and heat, sweat, and growth permeated the farm, he looked up one day from the field
of corn to see Elizabeth and Bryce driving down the
lane. Was it that they both seemed to sit more rigidly
than usual or that the hand she waved was more
formal, less flippant than usual? An anxious feeling
passed through him, a twinge in the stomach.

He finished what he needed to do and then, in his
rubber boots, carrying a shovel, walked back through
the orchard to the house, checking the peaches, pulling a couple of ripe ones to carry with him. When he
reached the house, he sat down on the step outside
and pulled off the muddy boots.

Inside, Noreen sat with the other two at the table.

"Father, Bryce received his draft notice." Elizabeth spoke as if she had seen the announcement of her son's death.

"Oh. Oh, dear." The ache was back in his stomach. His shoulders were suddenly very tired.

For his part, Bryce sat staring down at the table.

Noreen spoke slowly: "Daniel's going to come over. And Sally. Maybe Martha. I called her, but told her she didn't have to come, if she didn't want to."

Elizabeth spoke about her sister. "She has enough troubles, don't you think? Bobbie soon to be home at her house, in need of care. And Benjy going away soon. When Sis came back from Hawaii, she just looked beat up, mauled, but fierce in her determination to take care of Bobbie. I don't know if I could take it. I keep seeing myself in her situation, and Bryce in Bobbie's, and I think I'd rather go myself."

"They don't want you."

"I know...but I don't want them to have my son."

Noreen made coffee, and lemonade from a frozen can. She fixed a plate of sandwiches and set it in the middle of the table and put pickles and potato chips there. Opening a container of chocolate chip cookies, she placed them on a long narrow plate that had been Denver's mother's, and set it in front of the little group.

Still, Bryce said nothing, glancing around occasionally, an animal caught in the headlights. Sally came, and soon thereafter, Daniel.

The day was heating up. Denver closed the drapes against the rising temperature.

"I wish you wouldn't. I hate the closed in feeling," Noreen said.

"But the heat...You have to close them in the middle of the day. Otherwise the house heats up too much," Denver said.

"It's so dark in here," Sally said.

Elizabeth commented: "I'm in no mood for sunlight today. Usually I want them open."

"It seems kind of unreal," Noreen commented.

"We're usually outside most of the day, so you don't notice," Denver said.

"Is that what we came here for — to discuss the drapes?" Bryce said.

"No, of course not," Sally said, "but it's easier than what we came for."

"What are you feeling, son?" Elizabeth asked.

"Well, boxed in, I guess. I don't want to go. I'm not sure there is any point to this war. When it comes down to it, to put your life on the line, you need to believe you are fighting for something terribly important. Still, to not go means to become a criminal, to go to Canada, or to jail...I don't see any good choices here."

Everyone was quiet. He had put it so clearly there seemed little else to say. Denver thought he must speak. "It's hard to say this, son, but, your mother asked what you were feeling. I care about that. All of us here do, but as a country, if every young man made that choice himself, well, probably few would go. And America would have no defense. In the real world, how could that be? How can we remain a free country if no one is willing to put his life on the line? I don't want you to go, God knows I don't. Harold's death took Emma as well. I've always believed that's what killed her. Still, defending our country is sometimes necessary."

"You put it well," Daniel said.

"And, if it is so, then women should face the same challenge," Sally said quietly. "There's no reason we should get a free ride because we are female. I doubt that many even want to think about that."

Here, too, no one seemed to want to engage with that question. What had to be dealt with was more than enough.

"Seems to me that while a young man should be willing to fight for his country, he needs to believe what he's fighting for is important," Elizabeth said slowly. "Eisenhower warned us about getting involved in a land war in Asia. 'What is it for?' I keep asking, and I don't hear any answers that satisfy me. Meanwhile, our leaders argue with Vietnam negotiators over the shape of the 'peace' table. Is that what they're going to be doing while my son is out there being shot at?"

"Men have always just gone, haven't they, Grandfather? Harold signed up and lied about his age to go," said Bryce.

"Pearl Harbor had been bombed. Hitler was marching across Europe, determined to take over the world. Though it wasn't at first, it became a popular war."

"And this one isn't," Sally said.

"Every year we pray for peace on earth at Christmas, but it never seems to come," Noreen added.

"If we are to take an active role in peace coming, might it not be by refusing to go to war?" Elizabeth asked, looking toward Bryce, but not exactly at him, not wanting to confront him.

"Yes," said Sally, "Of course, in totalitarian countries, people don't choose their leaders, and when they're told to go and fight, they just do. So, if the free world chose not to fight and the unfree chose to be aggressive, well… the conclusion is pretty obvious. The U.N. is a good step, but…I don't know. 'What if there was a war and no one came?' Wonderful slogan, wonderful thought, but what if just one side came? They would be the aggressor, and they would roll over those who didn't resist."

"You're sounding more hawklike than I expected, Sally," Elizabeth said. "We are really talking about this war and my son."

"You're right, dear." Daniel put his arm around his wife. "Sally, when you go to Stanford, study and become a leader. We need people with your insights."

Bryce stood up, walked over to the closed drapes, opened them partway and looked out.

"Go ahead and open them, Bryce." Denver wanted the boy to see what was out there, to take it all in, to have this as something inside him, warm, real, and tender. Noting the young man's slender shoulders, the profile of his face that had seen so few whiskers, the white, clean hands, Denver thought of him as a vulnerable child and couldn't see him holding a gun, living in a swamp, or experiencing the horrors of war.

"Would to God they'd take me. I've had a good life. Bryce has only started."

Bryce opened the draperies and the brightness caused all of them to flinch or close their eyes until they had adjusted. He walked back to the table, picked up a sandwich, and began eating. The others followed him in this.

"Looks like you'll be harvesting that corn soon, Denver," Daniel said.

"Yes. Any day now. Probably tomorrow." Denver thought it unimportant at the moment. Elizabeth sat buried in thought and worry.

"When are you supposed to go to California, Sally?" Denver asked.

"A week from Thursday. I was so looking forward to the trip." Elizabeth had offered to drive her down and had invited Bryce and Noreen to go as well.

"It feels like an intrusion now. I feel so guilty because I don't face what you face, Bryce," Sally said.

"What he faces depends on what he chooses to do," Elizabeth said, again looking toward Bryce.

"Are there any real choices? Anyway, I want to go and take Sally to school, to see where she is. I don't have to report for almost a month," said Bryce.

"Then you are going to report?"

"I think so. I don't really believe in this war, but I don't like the prospect of running away. I can't say that I am doing it for my country — it's just too big an abstraction — but I can believe I'm doing it for this farm and this family. So Sally can make the world a better place."

"God, I hate this war." His mother began to cry. Daniel pulled a clean white handkerchief from the pocket of his suit, shook it out, and handed it to his wife.

"Maybe it will be over before he goes."

"Let's protest while we can, Bryce. And I'll join the rallies at Stanford. This means you won't be going to college," Sally said.

"Right."

"Moscow and the university will wait, son. We don't know that you'll even be sent to Vietnam. You're smart enough. You may get a desk job."

A car door slammed outside. Denver looked out to see Martha walking toward the house, plodding, though he thought it was not the weight of her body, but of her life, that made every step heavy.

Noreen greeted her at the door with a smile and a brief hug, and everyone else turned to say hello. "Come have something to eat."

Martha sat down and began munching on a sandwich. "So, another draft notice in the family."

"Yes. And, you just back from Hawaii. How is Bobbie?"

"He seems to be doing pretty well. He's on so many painkillers that it's hard to know. He sits up in a wheelchair quite a bit of the time. The whole trip and everything that has happened seem kind of unreal. Here we were, in this place that is so incredibly beautiful—the air is like a light swish of velvet.

The flowers…huge hibiscus, gorgeous bougainvillea, palm trees everywhere, and in the midst of this kind of paradise…Bobbie sits with an arm and a leg missing. He said to me one day, 'I still can't believe it. I keep thinkin' I'll wake one morning back in Idaho, whole, but I won't, will I? I'll be like this for the rest of my life,' and when he said that his tone was bitter and forlorn."

She sat looking down for a minute. Then she went on, as if she had to tell it all, had to say it to these family members. "Most of the time, Debbie and I visited him at different times. We weren't together very much, really. When she wasn't seeing Bobbie, she was on the beach or in the bars at night."

"She didn't say anything about Benjy, I'm sure, and you didn't either," Sally said.

"No and I don't want anything said by anyone else. Bobbie and Debbie seemed to get along pretty well — she spent some time with him each day, pushing him around in the wheelchair. As I said, I wasn't there at the same time she was. We agreed on when each of us would go. It was better that way. And she told me on the way home that it was over between her and Benjy, so, I think, in order to give Debbie and Bobbie a chance to make their marriage succeed, we best all keep our mouths shut. They are going to have enough challenges as it is."

"You're right, Martha," Noreen said and everyone nodded in agreement.

"They're going to live with me when he comes home. He has to be fitted for artificial limbs and he will need more schooling. It's gonna be a long haul."

A few days later, Noreen went with Elizabeth, Bryce, and Sally to California. Some of Sally's things had been sent ahead, still the trunk was full, and inside, cameras, snacks, pillows, and small bags filled every available inch.

"Do we look like hicks from the sticks?" Sally asked.

"Naw…well maybe a little. They find out this former waitress with no schoolin' is on campus, they might throw us off," Noreen laughed.

"Don't be silly. They would be lucky to have anyone with your brain—and heart," said Elizabeth.

The four of them stood alongside the car. Denver snapped their picture.

"You sure you'll be all right?" Noreen asked Denver.

"Course, I will. But don't you go thinkin' that I can get along easily without you."

"Well, it will be a nice change. I've never been to San Francisco or anywhere near it. Elizabeth thought we might come home through the Redwoods."

"Well take your time. See all you can. Come home and tell me about it."

When she came back a week or so later, she did. She could not stop talking. The places they had heard

about so many times had taken form before her eyes:
"Lake Tahoe. The cable cars in San Francisco. Didn't
think I could do it, but we just jumped up and held
on, Bryce standing next to me, kinda watchin' me
while we rolled down those hills! Why, I thought,
can't you just imagine this place in a snowstorm. I
know it doesn't snow there, but those steep streets are
scary. We walked across the Golden Gate Bridge and
saw the Rodin Sculpture Garden at Stanford."

She paused for a moment. Denver smiled watching her remember. She went on. "The sculptures, I
don't know how to explain it...I want to get a book
about Rodin at the library. I think those pieces will
stay with me for a long time. They are sort of like...
thought pieces, but also they must be felt." Her mind
moved here and there, tracing, connecting, and trying to pull it all together. Beyond that, finding words
to define that cohesiveness. He had known for a long
time that her mind was superior to his, had been
(shamefacedly) grateful, he supposed, that poverty
and place had limited her opportunities; otherwise
she would not have come into his life.

"Oh, it was hard to leave Sally. Her stuff that had
been shipped was there, so we helped her unpack
while Bryce wandered all over the campus, his eyes
as big as saucers. She planned it so when we had to
leave, she was on her way to an orientation meet-
ing, so we had to say goodbye quickly, still she could
hardly let go of Bryce, as if she had to memorize him.
Anyway, we drove that day to the Redwoods. We
were mostly quiet in the car. It was just the right place

to be, having left Sally. Oh, such magnificence! You should see them! Why your neck gets sore tryin' to see to the top. I took some pictures. I wandered alone for awhile. I've never felt closer to God. I think that is His cathedral. Somehow, being there takes you out of yourself. I was awestruck."

They lingered over dinner that night. After the dishes were finished, they went outside together. The corn had been harvested while she was gone. In the orchard, they found a few ripe peaches and plucked them from the tree to take back to the house and have later, topped with vanilla ice cream. The sun set low across the Owyhee Mountains. Insects buzzed.

He had run around all that day, changing the sheets on the bed and the towels in the bathroom, picking up newspapers and dirty clothes, running the wash, having everything clean and ready for Noreen's arrival. All seemed right, as right as it could be, now that she was here with him. Harvest upon them. Fruit ripening.

His contentment was with the land and the patterns of weather and this woman, Noreen, who loved him, and the feelings ran deep and full within him.

When they went to the bedroom, he watched her undress and sit in front of the mirror at the dresser, wanting her, flashing on how he used to watch Emma brush her hair. Chatting with his wife, he felt the delicious anticipation of having her body in his arms.

On a brilliant fall day, the sky clear and blue, the wind blowing leaves in the air, as if the world were jubilant, Bobbie returned home. Martha thought it best if everyone did not come to see him at once, so Denver and Noreen waited a couple of days, called to say they would like to come, and then went over. Noreen carried an apple pie she had baked. As was their custom, they rang the doorbell and then went in.

Entering the house, a smell hit their nostrils—something unpleasant, a mixture of medicine and cleaning sprays, possibly. The drapes in the living room were drawn, the room dark except for the light from the television set on its wrought iron cart across from the sofa. Bobbie sat in a wheelchair a few feet away from the television. A TV tray sat next to him with an assortment of drinking containers and medicine bottles. His head was slumped forward. He was perhaps asleep.

"Bobbie?"

The young man moved slightly, his hand moving to pull at the embroidered shawl across his lap. "Hullo, Granddad. Noreen."

"Son."

"Can I turn on a light? Or open the drapes?"

"Yes."

She found the string of the drapery and pulled it open.

Raising his hand, Bobbie covered his eyes a little.

"Is that too much?"

"No. It's all right. I'll adjust."

Denver reached the young man, put his hand on Bobbie's shoulder, then coming around in front, put out his hand. "It's good to see you." His voice broke and he was angry with himself, never having totally moved away from a childhood in which people didn't show emotion, particularly men.

Bobbie lifted his remaining hand, the left one, and put it in his grandfather's extended palm. "Yeah. Or what's left of me." Handsome still, his dark hair combed back, wearing the face of his father, the pain registered there in the slow, dull movement of his eyes, the lack of emotion on his face, and the monotone quality of his voice. The shawl, in various shades of green, lay across his legs, or what remained of them. He wore a short-sleeved shirt that buttoned down the front. Just below his right sleeve, the flesh ended.

He looked at the visitors as though it had been a long time — and worlds between — almost as if they were a memory. At the same time, he watched to see their reaction to him.

Noreen reached him, leaned over, and gave him a long hug and kissed him on the cheek. "We're so glad you're home."

"Yes, well, like I say, at least some of me is," Bobbie responded without enthusiasm.

Inside, Denver was crumbling. He needed walls within him, and some kind of machismo that he did not possess to face this disfigured young man.

"You're alive," said Noreen.

"Yeah."

"You'll be going to the Veterans Hospital for therapy and to be fitted with prostheses."

"Yeah. That's something to look forward to."

"We'll take you. We will do anything we can," said Noreen.

"Yeah."

"We won't feel sorry for you, but we will care for you and help you,' said Noreen.

"Okay."

Denver sat still through this exchange. Absently, he stroked his hand, the left one, where the finger was missing.

Bobbie looked at Denver's hand and said, "When I was a kid, I was always going to ask you about how you lost that finger. Mom said she didn't even know and that I was not to ask. Now, it seems...such a small thing."

"It is a small thing, though I didn't think so at the time. It happened at the sawmill. Guess I was lucky not to lose them all. I was holding a piece of wood. My hand slipped. I felt this awful pain and saw part of my finger fall off. I must have turned white and grown faint because Father handed me a handkerchief to wrap my hand in and let me sit down. He went right on working. I was dizzy and nearly fell off the chair — the blood coming through the handkerchief. Someone else, the wife of the owner I think, took me away, gave me some whiskey, and sewed up the wound. She must have given me a lot of whiskey, because I fell asleep. Some time later, my father shook me to wake me up, so I could walk to the wagon to go home.

"When we got home, Father had something else on his mind and that's what he talked about. He didn't mention the finger until Mother saw the bandage and noticed how pale I was. I remember her looking up at him and down at me, and then back at him, and sayin', 'You didn't stop to bring him home? That's hard, Joseph. That's very hard. You might have carried him in. You might have told me.' She had me lie down and found some ice and packed my hand so it didn't throb so much. She brought me soup and bread and for several days, she watched over me closely. It's about the only time I know'd her to say anything to Pa, and funny thing, he didn't say anything back. He, always so quick and full of authority, it must have been that look she gave him. He said nothing and let her coddle me without protest. Oh, he didn't change; he was soon as mean and bossy as ever. That's just how he was. The only other thing he ever said about it, a couple of weeks later, was, 'Proves you're a man. Makes people know you're tough.'"

"You've never told the story before," Bobbie said, coming out of himself a little.

"No."

"It's as much how others responded that you remember as the accident itself."

"Yes. But it is nothing compared to your injury, Bobbie. Still, you'll have good care and they can do so much for you these days."

"Much of it is still how people react to you—with pity or concern or like you're some kind of a freak. And what kind of life can I have?" He paused, looked down at his lap. "They say they can fix me up so I can walk and drive and do most things, but I don't know. Can't quite believe it until it happens."

"That's right. Is Debbie here?" asked Noreen.

"No, she went out. She's looking for a job, I guess."

"I hear congratulations are in order."

"How 'bout that? Guess there are still some parts of me that work."

That fall, as leaves turned brilliant yellow, pink, and red, and dropped from the trees to leave a skeleton of trunk and branch, Denver and Noreen prepared for winter by plowing the harvested fields, picking the orchard clean, and covering the winter vegetables with feed sacks.

The daylight hours grew short, the shadows, long. By three o'clock in the afternoon, the air was chilly--especially so in the heavily shaded areas.

"It's so still this year," Denver commented as he and Noreen put baskets and tools away for the winter.

"Yes. Sally gone. Benjy off to war, and Bryce to training. Bobbie home, but…so injured. It's a troubled time."

Elizabeth came out sometimes, to share her worry, or "just to be here." Sometimes Daniel came with her. "You never appreciate your parents until you have kids."

"Well, it will be good to have Sally home at the holidays."

"Yes. Seems like Alice has kind of grown up since Bryce left. She's taken her piano lessons and her studies more seriously. She said to me the other day, 'Momma, it's so quiet here without Bryce. You know, I always used to go to his room. He was studying and sometimes we didn't talk much, but it felt good to be with him. If I had a question about homework or somethin', he would help me. Other girls tell me how their older brothers can be so mean—and I guess Sally's have been sometimes. Bryce never was.' I said to her, 'Well, he'll be back.' She looked at me for a long time. 'Yes, Momma.'"

"This war," Noreen said, "I hate it. Martha calls sometimes, but she is really busy."

"Bobbie and Debbie living there can't be a picnic with all he must be going through. Did she tell you about Debbie?"

"Being pregnant? Yes. Seems to me there is some question as to who the father is."

Denver looked uncomfortable, but the two women went on.

"I think you're right. It happened right around when she went to Hawaii. Could they have...you know, done anything in the hospital?"

"Martha says they could, but she says Debbie was with Benjy right before she went to Hawaii."

"Little slut," Denver said.

"Don't let Benjy off the hook. He's just as responsible as she is," Noreen added.

"I 'spose, but it seems like women can control those things," Denver observed.

"Maybe they can, but both are equally responsible. Bobbie doesn't know about what happened. He thinks the child is his and he's rather proud of that. For him to be potent after what happened — it makes him feel like he is still a man," Elizabeth responded.

"We should not do anything to make him doubt that," said Noreen.

Noreen wanted to help Elizabeth prepare Thanksgiving dinner, so she and Denver went over early, driving the few miles through a landscape taking on winter at a brisk pace. Leaves clumped along the sides of the road or flew in the biting wind, dancing occasionally in an updraft, as if having someplace to go, some future, yet unknown. Trees grew bare, brown, and skeletal. Summer's fullness and green gone, the land took on shades of gray and brown. Darkness came ever earlier and in daylight, the sky was often dun colored. Dullness set in like a flat hand pressing down.

"I love it when it snows."

"Yes." In his mind, Denver saw big flakes drifting down, the clean whiteness covering the pallid ground, freezing in the trees, so bright and hopeful he might have to put on sunglasses. "I'll be glad when we get a hard snow."

"And no cows to milk, but you don't care much for that store-bought cottage cheese."

He grinned at her.

They drew up to the house.

"This year is hard for Elizabeth. Bryce training to go to war—it makes her crazy. She hates the whole thing," Noreen said.

"I know. We never seem to get away from it. Every generation..." Denver began.

"I don't know, dear. This one may make a difference. I'm not sure people will ever look at war quite the same," Noreen responded.

"Well, I hope our boys will be safe."

Alice greeted her grandparents. At fourteen, and since summer, she had begun to "fill out." The budding breasts embarrassed her. She wore a deep green velvet dress, full and long, so it covered her entirely. She loved art projects, and had brought numerous offerings to her grandparents through the years, colored-paper cutout valentines, Easter eggs, American flags in July—each with an unusual touch.

"Maybe...I don't know because I didn't raise kids of my own, but I think our Alice has some creative talent," Noreen had said to Denver.

Elizabeth came out from the kitchen, wiping her hands on her apron and extending her arms toward them. "Don't know what I would do without her this year. It's good to see you two."

Alice had decorated, bringing chrysanthemums, pumpkins, colorful striped gourds, leaves, and dried weeds into the house and arranging them at various spots. Place cards she had drawn contained a sketched profile of each person and identified where each one would sit.

Daniel was bringing in firewood. He took off his gloves, brushed his hands, and extended one to Denver, then kissed Noreen.

"A little nippy out there today. Think we'll be getting snow soon?"

The front door opened. Daniel's parents came in, arms full of various things — champagne and covered plates. Mrs. Robertson waved a finger at all of them and proceeded to the kitchen. Mr. Robertson handed some packages to Daniel and turned to close the door. A gust of wind blew through the house. Noreen shivered.

A little later, Martha, Bobbie, and Debbie arrived. Daniel's parents had not seen Bobbie since his return.

Daniel and Mr. Robertson went outside, greeted everyone, especially Bobbie, heartily, and carried the wheelchair up the short flight of stairs.

"You'll be up and going in no time," Mr. Robertson said to Bobbie. "Why they can do so much these days..."

"They can't give me back my arm and leg."

"But they have such good artificial limbs."

Mrs. Robertson came back from the kitchen. "They'll fix you up good as new in no time." She was tall with striking gray hair, a face taking on wrinkles, and a double chin; still she was a handsome woman, whose hands were rarely quiet. She had an efficient look, and seemed to judge quickly where things stood and what she needed to do to right them. She lost no time in turning to that purpose. "Right?"

Bobbie stared up at her.

"We will all help Bobbie do what is necessary to have a normal life, but good as new is…not possible," Daniel responded to his mother.

"Well," Martha turned to Bobbie, "here's a cushion for your back. Would you like anything to drink?"

"A beer, I guess, if you have one." Debbie got one from the kitchen.

"Come on, Debbie. Let's see what we can do to help the girls in the kitchen," Mrs. Robertson said, putting her arm around the younger woman and guiding her away. Debbie looked rather pretty. She had recently begun wearing maternity clothes. Her skin looked plump and healthy.

"I guess the Packers are on soon," Mr. Robertson said.

Daniel turned on the television. Denver and Mr. Robertson watched the game, Daniel joining them part of the time, when he wasn't doing something else.

"Hey, look at that pass, Bobbie."

Bobbie drifted off, then jerked suddenly, hearing his name called, looked about confused, and went back to sleep.

"Guess this is your quiet time of the year on the farm," said Mr. Robertson.

"Yes." Denver did not much like sitting on the couch, staring at the television. He stood and went out to the kitchen, smiling when Noreen looked up at him from where she stood, mashing white potatoes. The kitchen was bright, filled with activity, warmth, and reality.

Elizabeth engineered everything, checking the turkey, lifting a lid from a pot on the stove. "Alice, dear, have you filled the water glasses?" Alice responded that she had, "but the cranberry mold has to be taken out."

Martha stopped her restless finger tapping, rose from her seat on a high stool, and set to the task. She, too, was more comfortable here, without the pretense that seemed to go with the living room. She wore a straight wool tweed dress of mingled fall tones and she took time to put an apron over it before proceeding. Gray was beginning to show in her short, dark hair, near her face. She moved with ease, but without joy — the impact of Bobbie's new place in her life, as well as Debbie's and the expected baby's — an overwhelming situation.

"How's it going for you, Martha?" Elizabeth asked.

"Well, I have to admit I'm tired most of the time. It's a strain on us all. Debbie's out looking for a job;

being pregnant, she's tired when she gets home. Bobbie doesn't pick up after himself, and I hate to ask him, so when I come home at night, the house is a mess."

"Why do you hate to ask him?" Noreen wondered.

"After all he's been through…it seems such a trivial thing," Martha said.

"I'll ask him. We can't coddle him. He'll never do anything," Debbie said.

"You're right, dear. He needs to do things." Elizabeth was draining steaming water from a pan of sweet potatoes. "I think that's the toughest part—to recognize and sympathize with his wounds and pain, without doing it so much as to, sort of, excuse him from doing anything for the rest of his life."

"He's feeling sorry for himself," said Daniel.

"Which is understandable. Still, somehow you have to find a way to carry on. I know it isn't easy for you, Debbie," said Noreen.

The younger woman looked down. She was standing at the counter, her fingers pressed against it.

"It's not easy for any of us. I want him to move forward at the pace he's comfortable with," Martha said. "Just to have him back…the war haunts him. He doesn't sleep well, does he, Debbie?"

Debbie continued silent, perhaps a little embarrassed with the discussion. "I know you guys wanna help, but…I don't like talkin' 'bout all this, like we were freaks or somethin'."

Mrs. Robertson, who had remained quiet, now saw her opportunity to take charge. "You are absolutely right, my dear. "Lizbeth, let's get the food on the table."

"Yes, of course. Dad, would you like to carry the turkey?"

"Why, yes."

Though this year was a more somber Thanksgiving than most, the table was festive and covered with all the traditional dishes. The scents of turkey and mincemeat filled the air. Tall goblets glittered in the candlelight.

When they sat to eat, Daniel raised his glass to toast, "The family here and gone."

Then they joined hands while Noreen prayed. "Keep Benjy and Bryce safe, and bring them home soon. End this war. Help Bobbie to heal and be whole. Bless the new life in Debbie's womb. Take care of Sally at Stanford, and William and his family in California. We all need your care. Make us worthy of it. Thank you for each one around this table and for every good thing in our lives. Amen."

Denver thought it all an effort for Elizabeth this year, rather than a pleasure, though nothing in her actions or words would have told him that. Emma had gone about her work as before when Harold left, but he had occasionally come upon her in the middle of a task, just gazing into space. She had seemed numb, had gone about in a rote manner, as if she was not sure any of it mattered anymore. She paid less attention to little things. Wariness was always at the back of her eyes. Denver recognized some of this now in his daughter—that gut awful fear. What if he does not come back? How will I live?

Chapter Nine

1997

The intercom buzzed. Denver leaned over, pressed a button on the front of a small white box on the table. "Yes?"

"Granddad! I'm here!" Sally spoke through the machine, her voice like Lauren Bacall's, thick, full and laden with richness.

"Come on in!" Denver pushed another button that opened the door to the building. He reached for his cane and rose slowly from his favorite worn armchair. A kaleidoscope of memory tumbled around him. Sally the little girl, the assertive, yet caring teenager, her thin body like a straw in the wind, but her mind and spirit grounding her. When she spoke at graduation—what a day! After that, her successes took place at a distance—graduation from Stanford, two years in Malaysia with the Peace Corps, more school, becoming a political science professor, occasionally called in to talk on news shows such as the Lehrer News Hour on PBS. Now, she was a Congresswoman from California — elected last November. Through it all, always their Sally — oh, she could be a pistol, but she was warm and loving. Only one time had he been afraid for her. He turned his mind from that.

"It's a shame she never married," Denver had said just last night to Noreen as they walked the corridors of the retirement center. They had a small kitchen in their two-bedroom apartment, but took most of their meals at a communal dining room, and then frequently walked the entire perimeter before returning to their apartment.

The two-story building had a large, wide-open center, a lobby, with a ceiling two stories high. In this area were small seating areas with couches, chairs, tables, and plants. Along the walls, paintings by Idaho artists hung, featuring the varied landscapes of the state. The rugged snowy peaks of the Sawtooth Mountains. The wild Salmon River as it rushed through gorges and past forests. One, which Denver liked best, of his farmhouse, the land, and the Owyhee Mountains in the distance.

They often stopped in front of that one. He liked to lean forward and read the signature in the corner, "Alice Robertson." Several of her paintings were on display, and she had given her grandparents one for their apartment, which would move into the public area when they were gone. In it, she had painted the barn with straw on the ground around it. One upper window was open, banging in the wind. He could almost hear it. A tawny-colored Jersey cow stood near the barn, along with the figure of a man much like himself carrying a bucket.

"Seems like she took all that you and Emma said about the land—though she never saw Emma—and turned it into these pictures," Noreen said.

"It made it easier moving here—this painting and the others. That one of the picnic in the orchard. I love that." Turning to Denver's comment about Sally, "Yes. A couple of times I thought she would marry. Remember, we met an older man from France and another one she'd taught with?" Denver nodded. "Still, as long as she's happy…and she's certainly busy. I'm glad we have that second bedroom so she can stay with us, though I thought she might stay with her mother."

"Ah—well, too much pain there." They had been passing some large windows. Outside, the trees were beginning to bud and the grass was turning green. Spring was on its way. Beyond the lawn, he could see the gray arch of a freeway exit in its curve downward. Some drivers had turned on car lights. The beams flickered quickly past, following one another, reminding Denver of nothing so much as an anthill. He could see buildings, and more buildings in the distance, and the flashing neon lights of a business, seeming to say, "I'm here! Don't forget me!"

"Can't see the Owyhee Mountains," Denver had complained the first time they had looked out these windows. He mentioned it no more. He drew the undulating line of those mountains above the buildings in the skyline of his mind. "Just yonder, out there to the southwest, that's where the Owyhee Mountains are," he would say to whoever came by.

Now, with Sally coming, he made his way to the door.

"She's here!"

"I could get the door." Noreen came out of the bedroom, wearing a yellow pantsuit with a scarf at her neck. There was a small beauty shop at the center. Noreen had an appointment once a week. Her hair was still blonde. "But, I s'pose you want to."

"Yes." He opened the door and peered down the hall in time to see Sally turn the corner. With one hand, she pulled a suitcase on wheels with a second bag atop it, a computer probably. She waved with the other hand.

She was thin though not small of frame, and hand-some. Her thick, reddish-brown hair was pulled back softly. The lightly freckled face, with round cheek-bones, and large flashing eyes filled with excitement and purpose. She wore a business suit, though she had said on the telephone that she planned to don jeans as soon as she unpacked, and "not wear panty-hose during the entire visit." She had flown straight here from Washington D.C. for a few days of vaca-tion.

He had not thought of Emma for some time, until, watching Sally approach, he thought of her grand-mother, who had not been much older than Sally was now when she died. Emma, before the sickness took her flesh and her color, when she strode from orchard to flower bed to vegetable garden, pruning this, tending that. And the children — her world. Sometimes, he had noticed her weeding in the garden when a car turned down the lane. She would stand up, a hand going automatically to her side as if to alleviate the pain in her back. With the other hand, she shielded her eyes from the sun, so she could see who was coming.

When she was dying, Emma told him that she always dreamed that Harold would come back, light brown hair and easy smile running to her across the grass. So little of him came back — dog tags and a scrap of a family picture. He had no romance at the time — or ever, as far as his father knew — except that of going to war. Wouldn't it be nice if he had had a girl in England? He never mentioned one. A letter came. Denver had forgotten that. Emma had held it, reading it over, then setting the paper in her lap. She had looked out the window for a long time. She had answered the letter, but they never heard again. Evidently, the girl had moved on or had purged the ghost of Harold in the first writing.

Who had Harold been to anyone there? Denver had seen pictures in Life Magazine of the rows of white crosses, each one representing a loss to an American family like the one they had suffered. When Elizabeth and Daniel, along with William and Susan, went to Europe a few years ago, they had driven out from Paris to look at the Normandy beaches and the American cemetery, "trying to think what it was like for Harold that day," Elizabeth had said.

The dead remained with Denver, and would until his memory died. "Who's that?" the young ones would ask eventually, staring at a picture. Finding a faded letter dated January 2, 1902, or a large, beautifully carved silver serving spoon, they would want to know who wrote it or owned it, wanting to know the connection to themselves. "That belonged to your great-grandmother," someone who still remembered would say.

When he died, no one would be left who had known his parents — he was their last surviving child — seemed like that would be the end of them. 'Course, there would be stories. By the time Benjy's children, or any of the great grandkids, or another generation, told stories of Denver's parents, the tale would take on mythic proportions, "My great-great — I don't know how many greats — grandfather came west in a covered wagon, fought Indians, barely survived, homesteaded the land," they would say, mixing movie tale and truth in the telling.

These thoughts came to him frequently now. Both he and Noreen were still healthy, remarkably so, but he was 89 and Noreen would be 82 soon. They couldn't live forever. At one time, he thought he couldn't go on without Emma, but he had — to smile and laugh, even to be light, though not quite young again.

Emma had lived for those in her circle of concern, as did Sally, but the circumference of Sally's world was so much larger.

Sally's presence interrupted his memories.

They drew her in with hugs and kisses. Before they had finished greeting each other, she stopped suddenly, reached for something in her pocket, frowning, "My pager. It can wait. You two are looking good!"

"S'pose they never leave you alone. Somebody always wantin' somethin'." Denver said, smiling at her.

"True, but I am learning to pace myself. These first months, though…have to admit, I haven't had but but three or four hours sleep a night. But I'm here to relax and see you and the rest of the family. How are you?"

"Very well, my dear. Don't let this place fool you. It's not for the dying—at least the near to death. We are 'fully ambulatory,' something to be proud of in the senior world. All those things you learn to do as a child—go to the bathroom, feed and dress yourself—well, if you can still do them at our age, you are well off. And we can."

Denver chuckled. "So don't forget the basics, Sally, no matter how much else you have in that bright head of yours. Neither of us have had any major health problems. Oh, we watch our cholesterol and take vitamins, sleep more than we used to."

"What's this for?" Sally asked, pointing to the cane her Grandfather held.

"A bad knee."

"Have you considered replacement surgery?"

"No, not at my age. It's not really recommended."

"Well this is the first time I've been here, you know, so I'll need a guided tour. Senior services are getting more attention in the legislature all the time.

People are living longer. Seniors vote, and they have an active lobby. All of which you already knew. Sorry, sometimes it's hard to turn the political wheels off."

"We watched on C-Span when you were sworn in," Denver remarked.

"Very proud we were. I guess the AARP lobbies for the old folks. Right?" Noreen said. "I have mixed feelings about that bunch, though we belong. Sometimes it seems like the needs of the young are not given sufficient attention."

"You're right. The youngest can't vote and the poorest don't have a lobby. Money and politics… don't even get me started."

"All right you two, enough of politics, though I s'pose it is hard to get away from it when that's your job."

"Right…and I'll learn something about senior services while I'm with you that I can't get from reports and papers."

"Well, we haven't given you a chance to settle in — or change your clothes. I'm sure you'd like to do that. Here let me show you. We have a family dinner planned for tonight. Out at the farm. Everyone's invited. Even your father. We left a message, but haven't heard."

"Okay. I've made my peace with him…as much as can be made. Is everyone else coming?"

"Well, we don't know about your mother and Bobbie. They're not very well."

"You might want to call them."

"Are they hurt that I'm not staying with them?"

"I think your mother's relieved. She might not act like it, but they aren't in a position to have a guest."

Before long, Sally came out of the room, holding a telephone to her ear. She put her hand over the receiver and mouthed the word, "Mom" to them. "Hi, Mom. Yeah, just got in. How are you?" Silence again. Sally walked around the room, looking at every knick-knack, picking things up, remembering. "I hope you can come tonight, Momma." When she hung up the telephone, she looked discouraged. "Things don't sound good with Mom. I'm afraid she's become a victim. I know she's had lots of difficulties — Dad, then Bobbie, then her own illness, but…I'm going to go out there tomorrow. Have a look for myself. See if there's anything I can do. She just rattles off one complaint after another. She can't eat. She can't sleep. Can't control her bladder. Only place she ever goes is to the doctor. Then she waits forever to be seen, and when she is, doesn't get much attention. Do you see her often?"

"Can't say as we do."

"We've tried, but those two…both complain about their health and each other, and if anyone else says anything, they get defensive. Bobbie chain smokes — we both hate being around all that smoke--and takes way too many pills. He became addicted to pain medication when he came back from Vietnam. You never can tell what he's going to be like. Sometimes he's fine, but the next minute, he turns and looks at you, with this mad stare, his eyes not blinking and his face stern and unemotional, and you think, I don't even know this person."

Bobbie had lived with his mother most of the time since he returned from Vietnam. Debbie and the baby girl, Victoria, born in 1971, had lived there for awhile. That was no good. Martha and Debbie were always at each other. Bobbie and Debbie, fighting, making up, and then fighting again.

"So take care of the baby," Debbie had said "while I work." He had agreed, but the child got on his nerves. If she didn't cry, he neglected her, forgetting even to feed her sometimes. If she cried and fussed, he yelled at her, and finally struck the thin, pale child.

Martha, coming home unexpectedly one day when Bobbie did not hear her come in, saw him strike the little one.

"No. Never again. That's not going to happen to another generation." She gathered diapers, some clothes and toys for the girl, and taking her in her arms, drove her to Denver and Noreen's.

From their house, she called Debbie and told her what happened. "The baby is safe now, but she can't be with Bobbie. He's too sick to take care of a little one."

Debbie had filed for divorce the next day. She and the baby stayed with her parents, though Denver and Noreen took care of Victoria quite often, especially in the winter when the demands of the farm were less. They delighted in the child.

"She's pulling herself up on everything now." Noreen would tell Debbie when she came to pick up her daughter. "She's drinking better from the cup."

Debbie would smile.

One night Noreen asked Debbie if she'd like to stay for supper.

Shyly, Debbie agreed.

"So, how's your work?" Noreen asked, adding another place at the table. Slowly Noreen reached out to the younger woman, and gradually, Debbie allowed herself to be fed at their table and warmed at their hearth.

In time, Debbie had re-married. Denver and Noreen were among the small group invited to witness the ceremony. They had continued to look after Victoria, as she grew into a toddler, until she went to school. Then, they picked her up after school, and kept her until her mother came later to take her home.

Now a young woman, Victoria had attended Boise State University for a couple of years, then had quit and gone to work. The office job she took made it clear how necessary computer skills were, and she had gone back to school, working part time as well. She shared an apartment with several other young people and stopped in weekly to visit Denver and Noreen. She would come marching in, her hair the color and style of the moment, in Levis and tennis shoes, wanting to tell them of some incident from the campus. Victoria would be there tonight.

The issue of who her father was had never arisen, though Denver noticed that Benjy's eyes always followed the girl when they were together. He had helped pay for her college.

Denver, Noreen, and Sally sat in the living room of the apartment, catching up on family members, which brought up the past, which was never completely over. In each remembrance, figures, scenes, colors, and sounds flickered, engaging the trio.

Noreen turned to present plans. "Benjy and Marianne said they would take care of getting Martha and Bobbie."

"Benjy's done all right for himself," Denver smiled at Sally. "Maybe he's the only one who benefited by the war."

"How do you mean?"

"Well, seems like, he sort of grew up. Lost all that surliness. Came back, went to school, and started building houses. First thing you know, he's got a going business."

"You're right. I'm proud of my brother, and there was a time I didn't think I would ever say that."

"He certainly helped us with the farm. He and Ronald."

"I hear from Ronald quite often, usually by e-mail. We've worked together on some environmental issues. He's involved with saving the Redwoods."

"Wonderful young man. Goes a bit far—he thinks the dams should be taken out—wonder if he has any idea what this valley was like before irrigation?"

"Perhaps a bit idealistic for me, but I love him all the same," Noreen commented. "He had a hand in what happened with the property."

"Oh, really? I never knew just how all that came about."

"He came, you know, and stayed with us while you were at Stanford. He was just a kid, but he worked sun up to sun down that summer with me." Denver was remembering how the young lad would pull off his shirt, his bare back browning in the summer sun, the slender muscles on his back and shoulders growing strong while he shoveled dirt and hauled fruit. "Never had a more willing worker. And every once in a while he would ask, 'What's to become of this land when you can't farm it anymore?' I'd say, 'Well, do you want to farm it?' He thought about that for a long time, for years I s'pose', but then he got caught up in environmental issues. Like you, Sally, he's taken on greater concerns.

"Remember when everyone came for my 80th birthday? He commenced to talkin' with Benjy about the land. Eventually, Benjy bought the property at a fair price, which allows us to live comfortably the rest of our lives."

"Oh, good. I'm glad it worked out well for everyone. Will Alice and her family be there tonight?"

"Probably. Their life is chaotic. She said they would come when I called, but sometimes she forgets. Other times they show up very late. She's just one of these people who doesn't work on the clock. Good mother, though."

"I'm afraid I haven't stayed in touch with everyone in the last few years. It's good to find out what's going on and it will be great to see everyone."

"Back to Bobbie. How is he with Victoria?"

"Well, not too good. She goes over once in awhile and they do play their guitars together occasionally. Daniel took Bobbie for lessons as long as he would go."

"Yes, I was glad to hear he was playing."

"Victoria told me, not long ago, 'Might as well write my dad off. He's hopeless. Can't depend on him. Don't know where he will be — mentally — the next five minutes. Sometimes he can't even get through one song.' Then — I'll never forget this — she said, 'Was he ever whole?' I didn't know what to say. So I told her that he was a very young man when he went overseas, that he never quite got the chance to grow up."

"He had more chance than Bryce." Sally mentioned the name Denver had feared. "You know, when I went to Washington, first thing I did, before I went to the hotel, I went over to the Wall." Her voice lost its certainty. "I found his name: Bryce Harold Robertson, Jr., died July 12, 1971. I sat there for the longest time remembering him and wishing — oh, how I wished — that things had been different. I should have pushed him not to go. It was the hardest day of my life, well you know. I was home for the summer. Daniel called. Elizabeth couldn't talk. You were there by the time I got there. Elizabeth — I've never seen anguish like hers."

"I have. In Emma when Harold died."

"And in you when Emma died. It cuts so deep. Bobbie wasn't the only one left with permanent damage from that war. Elizabeth, too, lost an irreplaceable part of herself that day," Noreen said.

"That's what compelled me toward politics. His death. I thought, if I could work for peace, for a better world, it would help somehow."

"With the draft gone, young folks don't think about it the same. The Soviet Union gone."

"That's one of the most amazing things in my lifetime. This big enemy, the cold war, and now, it's gone."

"Yes, and new battles to be won. Oh it's so good to be with you. To remember with you. You've been this enormous anchor all through my life. Your love is always with me. Your presence. Your values. I needed to come here, to remember, and to say this to you."

Denver smiled as he looked at her, not trusting himself to speak. He felt a tear slip along the wrinkles of his face. Noreen, too, was quiet.

Finally Denver spoke, "Guess you start thinking 'bout things when you don't know how long you'll be around. Sharing my days with Noreen, seeing you, Sally. It's worth all the pain and the losses. I've been a very lucky man."

Chapter Ten

"I couldn't wait to see Sally," Victoria said when she came bursting into the apartment mid-afternoon, waving to greet the three of them. A ring dangled from her nostril and another from her upper lip, the lips covered by a dark, grayish brown shade of lipstick, her hair very short, greased, and "puke green," as Benjy called it. She wore a colorful vest that covered a thin garment underneath it, Levis, and heavy black shoes with wide, high heels. Jewelry hung from her wrists and neck in hot pink, black, and metallic blue. She spoke rapidly. "A Congresswoman in our family! They'd love to have you talk over at the college."

"Thanks, but I'm on vacation."

"But, I'd make so many points with my teacher. Like, it'd be rad!" She dropped a backpack on the floor and plopped down, her legs extended in front of her, arm flung over the back of the sofa, as if to cover and fill as much space as possible.

"How are you, dear?" Noreen asked.

"Great, Gram!" She jumped up and hugged Noreen and then Denver. "Hi Granddad! Hey—I got an interview with H-P and Micron. How about that?"

"You're graduating in…"

"Computer science. In two months. How's that… and they said it couldn't be done!"

"Who said it couldn't be done?" Sally asked.

"Very few women graduate in the field," Noreen said.

"Right, Gram. Some people just look at me or they hear I'm into punk rock and stuff, and they think like I'm one of those street people."

"Appearance counts for somethin'," Denver said. "Think 'bout that before you go to those interviews."

"You mean change who I am for those corporate guys?"

"You've said you don't like people judging you by your appearance." Sally turned and spoke softly to the young woman. "I'm a little unclear. Is what we see on the outside—is that you? Or is that what your friends think is cool?"

"I don't want to, you know, go corporate."

"We know you," her grandmother responded. "But those people don't, so they—we all, to some extent, judge by appearance."

"Maybe just tone it down a little."

"Compromise?"

"Yes."

"I s'pose you are good at that now, but did you compromise at my age?"

"No, not much." Victoria's aunt smiled at the comparison.

"And when did you start compromising? I've heard...how you spoke at graduation, saying your generation would change the world, would not accept old men sending young men to war."

"That's right. By the way, are the young men you know going to war?"

"No. Not many. My cousin, Denver—Benjy's son—signed up."

"Yes, he did. Over his parents' objections. My, how the world has changed since Bobbie, Benjy, and Bryce were young," Noreen said. "There is no draft. The Cold War is over. Your generation reaps the benefits of what Sally's generation did. They challenged war."

"True," Denver recalled. "Even McNamara now says they knew we couldn't win the Vietnam War. Amazing. Kids in the street and they changed the world. Some of it for the good, perhaps, but, seems like there isn't much respect left for anything."

"I'm not sure you're right, Granddad. Respect for authority and authority figures isn't automatic anymore. It must be earned," was Sally's comment

"Right, Sally," Noreen said, "and I think that's good and bad. When authority isn't questioned, it can and often does run amok, but if it isn't respected at all, that's a problem, too. I want the policeman and the school teacher to be respected."

"If the policeman isn't on the take, or stopping someone because they have a rundown car or because they're black, or if he isn't enforcing a law that is unfair, then I respect him."

"Whoa! The policeman doesn't make the laws. He enforces them, so if you think the law is unfair, you have to lobby to change it."

"Yeah, you're right. Like you said, respect has to be earned."

"And with so much access to information now, people think they know what's going on and can challenge the authorities," Sally said. "Some challenge because of knowledge, but I think more do for lack of respect. It started with Watergate. There have been so many scandals, and rumors. Much of what passes for information is wrong. Victoria — you need to be a smart gatherer of facts."

"Yeah, many of my friends don't trust anyone. They think everybody's out to screw 'em, so everybody has to take care of themselves. That's not how I feel, because I've had some good people in my life."

"That makes a difference doesn't it?"

"All the difference. Friend of mine the other day, does drugs, said to me, 'You got screwed over by your dad, didn't you?' I thought about it. I don't like my dad much. Feel kinda sorry for him, but the rest of the family…they kinda filled in the holes, you know. So, I said to my friend, 'Well, even if I did, there were always people around who cared about me.' 'You lucky sonofabitch,' my friend said."

"It takes a village…"

"Yes, family's terribly important. I don't like the people who try to stuff family values as they see them down our throats, but I know the value of family," Sally said.

Denver watched the usually smart and sassy Victoria engaged in conversation with Sally. Oh, he liked to stick his nose in every now and again, but most of the time he was content to watch and listen.

Deeply content with life, Denver knew, also, that he didn't fear death. In some sense, the things that were important to him were in good hands—not safe exactly—but cared for. He, along with Emma and Noreen—it would be hard to say which of the two women had more impact—would leave not only progeny, but a love of the land and the family. He would have to trust that the next generation would pass the things that mattered along to the younger ones.

He often felt tired and napped frequently in the afternoon. On a recent afternoon, he had said to Noreen, "I think my body's wearing out."

"I don't want it to end. I don't want us to end, but we must, of course, sometime," Noreen said.

"But it's a good end. The crops are in. The cattle are fed. There's food in the larder. It's that satisfaction at the end of the day. It's a good tired."

He came back to the conversation.

"Look at Ron's work for the environment. Before about the '70s, no one thought about recycling or preserving resources for future generations. Our consciousness has been raised in a number of areas."

"True," Denver said. "Ah-h, it's all too much."

"Life seems more complicated now," Noreen said.

"There was a time when everyone knew what was right and wrong. Or we thought we did." Denver smiled at the three women. "I guess old folks tend to see the past like…I don't know…like Alice's paintings. The impression stays with you. It's what you are used to. Then young folks come along and ask why and you don't want to be bothered with explainin' it. You want to say well, it just is. It's a good thing young folks question things."

"You're right, dear. And I've read all these things about the rate of change increasing so much in our lifetime."

"Seems to me you two have done a marvelous job of honoring the past and accepting the future — like Victoria here." Sally turned to the young woman. "Do any eyebrows go up out there when you come to visit?"

"Yes, they do. First time I came, someone called security."

Denver and Noreen smiled.

"Victoria came in and helped all of us in the computer center. We can get e-mail down there now, you know, Sally. Most of us are too old to really get into computers, but getting e-mail helps us stay in touch. Victoria set that up and worked with us until we could do it for ourselves."

Sally looked toward the younger woman with new respect. "When you interview, make sure you tell them about that. That's great."

"So you think I'm more than just a pretty face?"

"Much more."

"I'll see you guys out there. I've got to do a couple of things on the way," Victoria said.

Later that day, Denver, Noreen, and Sally drove out to the farm. They wanted to go while it was still light. Sally was at the wheel. They all shook their heads at the development going on in the valley, the new houses that stretched farther and farther into what had been farmland.

They left the freeway at Meridian, driving south. A few miles away from the bustling interchange, they saw a farmer driving a tractor, tilling the soil. Light puffs of dirt followed in his wake. Then they drove down the familiar lane, now paved and smooth.

It wouldn't be the same without the ruts in the road, without worry—would the truck run, would it get stuck in the mud, would the seeds get planted in time, would the weather hold? Farming came back to Denver as an endless and nerve-wracking concern.

The line of trees the neighbor had planted stood alongside the lane, moving in the spring breeze, just beginning to leaf.

"Ah-h, memories," Sally murmured.

Denver was getting a bit hard of hearing. At dinner, it seemed like everyone talked at once. He couldn't make out everything he heard. It mattered little. "Don't have to talk," Denver told Noreen. "Just to be here is enough."

Marianne had extended the dining room table with all its leaves to seat the family. After greeting his sister and grandparents, Benjy had gone to get Martha and Bobbie. There had been that awkward moment when he returned with them. Sally had gone forward to greet them. Her mother was in a sour mood and an unpleasant odor entered with her. Her thick gray hair was unkempt and dirty. Strands fell forward into her mouth. Her heavy body was swathed in blankets. Over her shoulders, a thick shawl had been wrapped. She had not raised her arms from the wheelchair to hug her daughter and barely responded to the embrace that Sally bent to give her.

"Can't you fix Medicare? I can't see the doctor when I want. My pills cost $300 a month! Takes forever to settle things! Do something, girl!"

Sally visibly blanched at the criticism. She turned to greet Bobbie. Hollow-cheeked, unshaven, and wild-eyed, Bobbie looked at Sally as if she were a stranger. His corduroy pants were worn and dirty, as was the flannel shirt that covered a white—now gray—T-shirt. He wore slippers. Though he did not smoke here—he would slip away numerous times to stand outside and light up—the smell came with him in clothes, hair, and breath. The hand he extended toward his sister was blue-veined, shaky, and thin. She ignored the hand and pulled him forward in a large hug.

"Hi, Dad," Victoria entered, "Hi, Grandma."

"H-hello, sister, Victoria." Bobbie was teary eyed from the embrace. His emotions fluctuated rapidly.

Sally took his hand, led him forward to a chair, and sat down next to him. She held his hand, saying nothing.

"Where's Elizabeth?" Martha asked.

"Oh, she'll be along shortly. So, how are you?" Noreen responded.

"Half the time, I wish I were dead. Don't know what keeps me goin'. Something in my colon now. They're lookin' into it! By the time they decide what it is and what to do about it, I'll probably be a goner. Haven't seen you for awhile."

"No, we haven't been out much this winter with the icy roads and all."

"Be getting' out a bit more now that spring is comin'." Denver was appalled by the look of these two, the dirt and stink of them. Probably, he had given up on them, though he hated admitting it. He was sorry for Martha, and regretted that it seemed so beyond his power to help her—as if he had somehow given her a fatal flaw and could not erase it.

He and Noreen had talked about Martha and Bobbie many times, trying to think of the best way to help them. In the early years, they went over to spend time with Bobbie, to take him to the doctor, or play cards with him, or simply visit, and while he did not lash out, as Martha did, he was simply vague, almost absent.

"Maybe if Debbie had stuck it out," Noreen said, "though I can't blame her for leaving. You know, from the time he came home, Martha told him, 'You're sick. You're an invalid. You'll have to stay here with me the rest of your life.' He tried in those early years, getting married again, working. Martha clung to him, hung on to his need, his weakness. She made it too easy for him. He didn't have to have a job. Gradually the two of them were pulled into this mire, where they drag each other down."

Benjy—probably they should call him Benjamin now—was quite different. At 47, his dark hair was neat and fell forward softly, not so rigidly held in place as it had once been: handsome now, more so than either his dad or brother had been, muscular, and fit. It must be the confidence. He wore gray flannel slacks and a silk shirt, and seemed comfortable with himself. So much pain had come from that war. Denver had been pleased to watch Benjy come home more sure of himself, grateful to be alive and energetic to make the most of it.

Three years after Benjy came back, Denver and Noreen had witnessed his marriage to Marianne, an athletic young woman with a wide face and full figure who shared his enthusiasm for living. Unassuming and sometimes unthinking, she was outspoken, had the natural directness so often admired and quite typical of Idahoans, even when the statements she made were based on scant knowledge.

Noreen had dubbed Marianne, "our Martha Stewart," and the younger woman did indeed excel in domestic skills. She had supervised the remodeling of the place once Denver and Noreen had moved out. She spent hours talking with Denver about how the house was when he was a child, looking at old photographs and letters — treasuring any scrap from yesterday.

Determined to preserve whatever remained original at the farm, she studied restoration techniques assiduously, reading, taking classes, going to the East Coast once with Benjy to look at restored homes. The old barn, now known regionally because of Alice's paintings, looked just as it had, repaired with methods that did not change its appearance.

Denver and Noreen drove out to the place occasionally, Noreen at the wheel. Driving down the paved lane, the orchard came first into view. Wide porches had been added to the two-story house. Wicker chairs and settees sat here and there, bringing a graciousness that the house had always lacked when they lived there.

"What do you think?" Benjy asked his grandfather and Noreen before adding the porches.

"It's all right. Seems to me each generation makes its changes."

"Without screens," Marianne added.

"Absolutely. Leave it open, so nothing slows your view across the valley."

Marianne had opened the old shed and cellar, cleaned them out all together, preserved and repaired the old wood, scoured the concrete and stone cellar, and had Benjy add electricity to the shed. She brought out old tools, a large wheel, which Denver told her, "was part of the buggy my father used to drive"; rakes, hand or horse-drawn plows, and milk cans. She handled each piece lovingly, carrying the dust-covered canning jars from cellar to kitchen, washing them in hot, sudsy water, her fingers tracing the raised glass line of the words "Kerr," "Ball," or "Mason" on the quart jars.

She found the pressure cooker Emma had used and canned peaches, cherries, and pears picked from the orchard. She made preserves and new concoctions Denver had never known. The filled jars were on a shelf in the cupboard, in a drawer Denver had slept in as a newborn. It sat open in the living room. Family pictures, quilts, a child's crocheted booties, a black-edged envelope announcing the death of Denver's mother, a pocket watch. All of this flowed from shelves that were part of the yesterday Marianne sought to preserve.

The large pieces of farm equipment — the tractor and an Oppel Harvester, had been cleaned too — the rust removed and a new coat of paint added.

Marianne had turned her energy to the farm as her children grew and demanded less of her time. Their oldest son, Denver, had often been at odds with his parents — his father in particular. "He seems to bring out the least handsome side of Benjy," Noreen said.

Young Denver, now stationed at Fort Benning, Georgia, had been encouraged by his father to join the military, at a time when the young man's life seemed aimless and Benjy knew that he was becoming involved in drug use. Seventeen-year-old Jody was planning to attend the University of Idaho in the fall, while the youngest daughter, Jolanda, was in junior high.

"Sally works on tomorrow," Noreen had said to Denver, "while Marianne's efforts go to yesterday."

Sally and Marianne were talking now, leaning forward, and Denver wondered what they said. Still, they seemed to find more in common than Sally found with her mother or Bobbie.

Chapter Eleven

Part of a fax written by Bobbie, found later:
"I just went downstairs to check on Mom and the house is a mess and she is asleep. This seems so bizarre and sick to think you could murder your mother and then kill yourself but it would solve a whole bunch of problems in the future for the rest of you just to get it over with once and for all."

After Bryce died, Daniel had made it his mission to help Bobbie, and that in practical rather than emotional ways. He knew what kind of training was necessary to become a bank teller, and arranged for Bobbie to acquire those skills as a trainee at Daniel's company. Daniel had driven to pick up his nephew and take him for the schooling.

"How's it going?" Denver had asked Daniel.

"Oh, not very well. He was cleaned up and ready the first day, but the second he wasn't ready for a half hour after I got there. He's sick quite often. They tell me he's not very attentive and often is belligerent to the instructors. I talk to him about those things. I don't know what else to do. You know the saying, 'You can lead a horse to water, but you can't make him drink.' Well, that's how I feel sometimes."

"That's too bad. He should appreciate what you're doing for him. Wonder why he doesn't seem to."

"As much as anything, he lost any drive he had in Vietnam, any real energy to live, and that's hurt him more than the loss of limbs."

Noreen had commented, "Those two things aren't separate. He sees himself as less than whole. The war sucked the life out of him."

"I think you're right. He sits in this class where they teach you how to use a calculator, and so forth, and I guess he thinks, 'what's this got to do with anything?' After you've been in combat, everything else must seem mundane," Daniel said.

"He's not stupid. He ought to know a job makes him independent of his mother, able to live on his own, buy things, go places, perhaps have a girlfriend."

"You would think he'd see that. I said to him one day, 'Don't you want to live on your own?' He looked at me blankly and finally mumbled, 'Yeah,' and I think the desire is there, but perhaps it isn't strong enough to make him stick with things. Well, if this fails, I'll try something else, but it's discouraging."

Bobbie had rallied for a time, had taken the job training more seriously. The bank had hired him. He walked quite well and was able to do his job, though he tired rather quickly. He enjoyed being around people and told his grandfather there was "a girl at the bank I'm kinda sweet on."

After he worked there for a few months, he proposed moving to his own place, suggesting this one evening when Denver and Noreen were visiting at Martha's house.

"How would you manage?" Martha said. "I fix your meals and do the laundry. Clean the house. How are you gonna do all those things?"

"He'd manage," Denver said.

"The house is so empty without you. I have the rooms…might as well use them." Martha glared at her father. Then she closed her mouth, pursing her lips into a pout, folding her arms tightly across her breasts, and looked away, as if to say, "It's settled then."

No one said anything for a time. Then in a meek voice Bobbie began, "If you want me to stay…I thought it'd help you if I was gone."

"It's not me that needs you."

"Well, then, I might start lookin'."

"We'll help you move, Bobbie," Noreen said, "When you've found a place…"

"We'll talk about this later," Martha said.

"Thanks, Noreen. I'd appreciate that."

"I said," Martha spoke slowly as if chipping each word from stone, "We'd talk about this later. I won't hear one more word about it now."

She stood up, her angry mouth in place, and began picking up cups and glasses, clanking the pieces together, bumping her knee. "It's time for you to go to bed, son."

Bobbie had looked with helpless entreaty toward Denver and Noreen. They left soon, but determined to help Bobbie become independent. One day, they broached the subject when Martha was not at home.

"I don't think she wants me to go. She gets mad every time I bring it up. Michele, at the bank, we've dated a few times. I'd like to have my own place."

"It's better for you both if you make the break."

"You might have to just endure her wrath for awhile. We'll stand behind you."

"Thanks. I guess you're right. Enduring her anger isn't easy, though. She cares a lot about me."

"Yes she does, but she doesn't see the need for your independence. She likes having you around. Let me suggest something," Noreen said. "I wouldn't normally recommend this, but don't say anything to her. Find a place. Make all the arrangements and then tell her at the last minute. We'll be there with you, if you want us."

"Good idea."

"Thanks. I'll do it." He was driving again. He could check out apartments on his way home from work. He had looked hopeful then, a glint in his eye and a little grin on his face.

"I hope this works," Denver had remarked to Noreen as the two drove home.

"Oh, yes. I'm optimistic for him for the first time since he came home. What is it about Martha? Why does she so oppose this?"

"I dunno. My mother never wanted me to leave and I never did."

"I know, but there was a reason—someone to run the farm. The others had left."

"And someone needed to look after them as they got old and feeble."

"I heard someone on television the other day talking about the empty-nest syndrome—something about parents who don't know what to do when their children are gone."

"And lots of parents can't wait 'til they leave."

"Right. With Martha's husband gone, Sally and Benjy gone. Doing their own thing. Benjy didn't spend two nights at his mother's when he got home. Seems like she's clinging to the last one."

Back at the family dinner, Bobbie sat and seemed alone. He said little, responding only in the most cursory way to questions. His food was left mostly untouched.

"Take your pills, Bobbie," Martha yelled across the table. He fumbled around until he found a box in his back pocket—a weekly organizer for his pills—and dumped half a dozen tablets and capsules in his palm, then swallowed them between sips of water.

Alice and her family arrived. She had been married to Hau Soun for ten years, though she had not changed her name. Her light-brown hair fell loosely around her shoulders. She wore no make-up. The soft features of her face bore a kind of tender and sensitive beauty that needed no enhancement. She wore Levis, a dark purple turtleneck top, and over it, a richly embroidered vest in multiple bright colors — the yellow of a hot sun, the red of a fallen leaf, the green of new grass.

"What a gorgeous vest," Sally said as she stood and moved to embrace her niece, rekindling the warmth and regard these two had always had for each other.

Sally turned to greet Hau and the children. Maria, nine, and Steven, seven, had the physical characteristics of Eurasians. Maria was small-boned, delicate, with black eyes and hair. Freckles dotted the crown of the cheeks on the fresh, round face.

Steven's face was round as well, his hair lighter than his sister's, and he was already taller than his sister, something he took pleasure in pointing out to her frequently. He was running now, to jump into the arms of his grandparents.

Elizabeth and Daniel visibly brightened with the arrival of Alice's family. Taking delight in being grandparents, they visited and cared for the children often, tumbling around on the floor when the two were babies, holding, feeding, diapering — whatever was called for, they did with joy.

"I'm so glad Elizabeth has those new babies," Denver had said to Noreen.

"Yes. She's such a strong and good woman. You know, she said to me one day: 'I'll never get over losing Bryce, still these babies, they're a fresh wind. A new hope. I can use that.' And I said to her, 'Losing someone we love dearly should teach us to savor every moment and every good thing in our lives.'"

"Two wise women." Denver smiled.

Daniel had retired. Now, he volunteered two days a week at the Veterans Hospital in Boise. He and Elizabeth would be celebrating their forty-fifth anniversary this year. They still liked being with each other, arguing fiercely over a word in Scrabble, smiling at their private jokes.

Elizabeth had her arm around young Steven now and was smiling softly at the towheaded boy. She had not smiled for so long after Bryce's death that Denver had feared she never would again.

Sally and Elizabeth had been encapsulated in pain and grief after the news, clinging to each other that hot July day at the cemetery, sitting at his graveside as if life itself was gone and no tomorrow. Denver and Noreen worried about both of them. He shuddered now to think of that time.

Elizabeth fell two days later, on the front steps of her home — steps she had skipped, run, dashed, and walked for years. Possibly, shock from her son's death caused her to forget some tiny piece of those seemingly automatic movements. While the broken leg mended, a scar remained on her left cheek where her face had hit the pavement that day. Daniel had asked if she wanted plastic surgery. She had run her fingers across the ugly line. "No. This is connected to Bryce somehow. He lost his life. Mine will never be the same again."

She'd struggled after that. She told her father about the day she went with Daniel to pick up Bobbie, but Bobbie had not been ready. The drapes were drawn, dirty dishes and papers littered the living room as well as the kitchen. Bobbie had apparently forgotten he was supposed to go at all that day. Elizabeth automatically began picking up. Daniel looked uncertain.

"Damn you, Bobbie! You're alive. Can't you make something of yourself?" Elizabeth stormed.

"I don't think so. I can't think of anything I want to be."

"I wish Bryce had what you have."

"You'd rather he'd come back like this than dead? Well, his struggle is over. You'll always see him as this fresh, young man with the world open to him. You don't know what his life might have been had he come back as I did."

"No, I don't. You can breathe, eat, see the world, laugh, cry, and move about. You can do most anything you want to bad enough. Bryce has none of that. Why aren't you grateful for what you have?"

"Well, I...I suppose I should be, but I feel like a freak. That's how other people see me. I guess...the only things I succeeded at before I did with my body. Played football and basketball. Chased girls and, you know..."

"I don't think there's anything wrong with you in that department," Daniel said. "You're still a good-looking young man."

"A cripple."

"But you're alive! As long as you are alive, you can do things," Elizabeth said.

"I know, Aunt Lizzie, but...somehow, I don't have the will, or maybe just the energy or desire, strong enough to stay with it. I could tell you that I do... that I will, and make you feel good for the moment, but every time you come over here like this, you'll be disappointed again. I'm trying to be honest."

"Bobbie, it's so hard to hear you give up. I'm not ready to give up on you. I want to help you. I want you to succeed."

"Yes, I know you do. I feel you reaching for me, but..." Bobbie left the sentence and the outcome vague.

"You aren't the only one who is wounded here," Elizabeth remarked sadly.

Michele had come along and given Bobbie a new interest in life. Denver and Noreen met her one evening at the café where Noreen had worked so long ago. Now it was open for dinner, and they occasionally went to indulge in the "comfort food" served there.

They had just ordered when, looking up, they saw a woman of average height and weight with short curly blonde hair, brown eyes, and a pretty round face, leading Bobbie into the café.

When Bobbie saw his grandparents, he waved, mumbled something, and the pair came over to the table.

"Bobbie—nice to see you."

He introduced them to Michele.

"May we join you?" she asked. The older couple readily agreed.

"I work with Bobbie. After we got off work, I helped him look for an apartment and then decided to catch a bite here. We found something, didn't we, Bobbie? A one-bedroom apartment not three blocks from here, cute as a bug."

"Yeah."

"Good."

"It's partly furnished, so he wouldn't need very much. There's a couch and a bed. Everything in the kitchen. That color in the bathroom is awful. We'll have to change that. I may have some peach paint left over at home." Michele signaled the waiter. "Do you know what you're gonna have, Bobbie?"

Denver had wondered who was moving into the apartment.

"And where is home?"

"Right here in Kuna. My kids and I live 'bout a mile out in the Winters' house," she said, glancing at the older couple who nodded that they were familiar with the house. "My divorce is almost final. Rodney is this creep who promised everything before we got married and hasn't held a job since. My folks help out. They live over in Boise. Bobbie, do you wanna share that pot roast? Are you gonna have a salad? If you do, I'll just have a bite."

"Fine." Bobbie nodded and smiled at Michele and then at his grandparents.

He knows, Denver said to himself that he is being led, but he does not mind. Martha, however, will. Martha did.

Elizabeth had surprised them all in the way she had faced her struggle over Bryce's death.

"Her heart is broken," Noreen said to Denver, "And yet, she reaches out to us and to others."

"Maybe that's how it heals."

"Yes. You're right. The living should cherish each other. Elizabeth gets that and Bobbie never will."

"Sounds very final."

"I hope I'm wrong."

"I do, too." Denver didn't think she was. He didn't see Bobbie rising to battle the odds.

As the years went by, everyone's hopes for Bobbie diminished, though there were periods of optimism— his relationship with Michele the most promising. The job at the bank lasted for a year and a half, the longest time for any position. After that, he did not stick with anything--classes, work, or support systems set up specifically for veterans. He got a check from the

government. Though he could walk, he bought a motorized wheel chair, and a ramp was built at the front
of the house so he could come and go on his own.
Sidewalks had been built in the area around Martha's
house and he could ride to a small shopping center
three-quarters of a mile away.

Martha continued working at J.C. Penney's, but her
involvement with the chamber of commerce declined.
She dropped two other clubs, rushing home at the end
of each day to fix supper for Bobbie, glad — in some
secret part of her, to have her son there.

"Sally doesn't need me," Martha had said to her
father and Noreen one day, "neither does Benjy, but
Bobbie…well, he has a tough time."

"Martha, Bobbie wallows in self-pity. Don't let
your need allow him to avoid the struggle."

"What do you mean? Everything he does is a struggle. Just to get out of bed in the morning…"

"Your acceptance of him as permanently wounded
and unable to be on his own makes him so."

"I don't understand you. I do all I can for him.
You've never borne a child. You don't know. You're
just a step-mother."

"I suppose not…" Noreen felt sad that Martha had
pointed out her childlessness as somehow a failure.

"Maybe you do too much for him. Anyway, there's
no call for you puttin' down Noreen," Denver had
said.

"I'm tired of other people telling me what to do. I'll
do what I think best for Bobbie and me."

Denver and Noreen had watched Martha's slow decline in health and ambition, as the years went by — of coming home to Bobbie's glazed eyes that did not turn from the television set to look at her when she entered. The discards of what he had eaten — candy wrappers, paper containers that had held French fries, or Kentucky Fried Chicken — dropped about the room. Several overflowing ashtrays always dotted the room. In addition, cigarette burns were visible on tables, even the couch, the brown line an inch long in some cases, evidence of one being lighted and forgotten.

Martha wanted him there, but hated the mess that greeted her each evening. She came to resent his unwillingness to pick up after himself. Having this semi-invalid in the house caused her to lose sight of purpose or hope or reason for tomorrow.

Coming home, she would move around the room picking things up. "Can't you even take care of the things you drop?" Sometimes he answered. Sometimes he was silent. When she flew into a rage, he did a few things for the next few days, but that effort soon declined and he was back to his soaps. He followed those lives on screen as if they mattered, bought magazines that wrote about the series. They seemed the only thing he really cared about. He began taking on the personality of people on the screen, copying their gestures and words, or buying a hat or gloves so that he might affect the role that he had watched. He became furious if some world crisis interfered with his programs, calling the station, cursing whoever answered the telephone.

"Get a life," Benjy had said to his brother once, but for the most part the two had nothing to say to each other, no common ground, not even Sally's success, her books doing well. Bobbie did not celebrate anything that went well for others.

"He's drowning in his own shit," Benjy told Denver one day, "And he's enjoying the flavor!"

Denver turned away in disgust from Benjy's words, but he knew that it was true. "And takin' his mother with him, I'm afraid."

"Or is she taking him?"

Since that time, Elizabeth had confessed to being angry with Bobbie and his lack of goals or ambition to the point that she did not want to see him.

"It seems an enormous mistake that he lived and Bryce didn't," Noreen had said.

Denver looked at Elizabeth now as she stroked her grandson's head. She had poured all the hope and affection in the direction of Alice's children, caring for them regularly so Alice could paint, having one of them sleep over frequently, laughing and reading with them.

Hau Soun was bent over talking to Victoria, saying something about computers. "Alice uses a Mac. It is really best for anything artistic or graphic. You might talk with Sarah. She's with Sun Microsystems. She might be some help in getting a job."

"Great idea. I'll have to get her number from... someone."

"Pretty cool outfit, Vickie." Alice smiled at her niece. "Are you going to stay here? You would probably fit in with all those computer geeks in Silicon Valley."

"Well, I might. I dunno. How would I do in the Bay Area, Sally?"

"Well...it would be a big change for you. Whether you would like living there, I can't say. All those years ago, it was a big adjustment for me. Now it's home and I love it."

"I remember you coming home that first Christmas. Looking a little starved for us — for family," Elizabeth said.

"You sat over at our house one night," Daniel said, "We toasted marshmallows in the fireplace — something Lizzie wasn't sure we should do — and drank cocoa, and heard about Stanford from you. The 'farm' as you called it, though it wasn't the farm we all knew. Bryce was home on leave, pummeling you with questions. Did you have a boyfriend? Did you have to study hard? I think none of us wanted that evening to end."

"No, we didn't. Sometimes it seems the good times come and go so fast while the hard, unpleasant things stay on forever." A look of solid pain crossed Elizabeth's face.

Denver winced when he saw and remembered that time. The Christmas after Bryce's death had been practically unbearable, the death hanging over them, a fresh, bleeding wound.

On this evening, Martha's only compliment of the evening was when she said, "Lizzie, you got a good man, always stuck with you through thick and thin."

"Of course you're right," Elizabeth responded. "I was speaking of events, like this tonight. How quickly the time comes and goes. As I get older, I know how important the good times of sharing are."

"Now if I'd had a good man. One that supported me, well I'd wouldn't a' worn myself out takin' care of Bobbie and workin' and all." With this, she pulled out a large, dirty handkerchief and coughed repeatedly into it.

Benjamin, Sally's father, had not come that evening — no surprise. Sally stayed in touch with him and would see him while she was here, but Denver knew the family dinner could be awkward for his former son-in-law.

Martha's disposition, in recent years, had turned surly and cranky. Those gathered tried visiting with her, but with her steady complaints, they slowly moved away from her, taking up new conversations. Bobbie was picking at the old jacket that he wore, pulling at the right cuff, turning it over, and doing it again. Did he know the rest of them were there? Did he take note of the conversations that whirled around, but not through him?

Sally turned back to Victoria. "You were asking about the Bay Area. I love it. 'Course, I've been there, what? Twenty-seven years now. If you decide to come there, Sarah could be a big help. I would do what I could, but I just want you to know that it's different. There's so many more people, millions in the Bay Area alone, while here you have...maybe a million in the entire state. You can get lost and, I have to tell you...many people would look at the way you're dressed tonight and assume you're part of the drug culture. Sometimes you get no second chances. You have to be careful. I'm starting to sound like a mother."

"She knows what she's talking about, Vickie," Elizabeth said.

"What do you think, Pops?" Victoria asked.

Bobbie stared back at her with a puzzled expression. He had not lived with his daughter since that early time when Martha had taken her away. Debbie and her new husband — Bobbie referred to him that way though the couple had been married some twenty years now — had raised Victoria. She had remained close to her grandparents and to Elizabeth's family.

"Dunno," Bobbie muttered, raising a thin arm and raking his fingers through his hair. His finger touched something there — some bit of dirt or scab — and he pulled it out and turned his attention to figuring out what it was.

Involuntarily, Victoria shuddered. Bobbie knew he revolted his daughter. He looked wildly around the room. The artificial limb that was one of his arms flew into the air. It was as if he was winding himself up to speak. "Lizbeth, I wish I'd died instead of Bryce. Wish I could a' done that for you. Bryce'll always be this perfect young man. Instead, you've had me and I was never perfect. Never been a father to my daughter. Never done nothin' right."

"You are too hard on yourself, Bobbie," Elizabeth said.

"Am I? Look at my sister, the congresswoman. My brother, the successful entrepreneur. My grandparents, healthier than me. Certainly happier. Don't know what I got to get up for in the morning."

A pained silence spread across the group; then Martha spoke. "Boy, you ain't got nothin' on me."

"Least I never left you, Momma. You always wanted me home. After I came home from the war, you said I'd have to stay. You said nobody ever stayed with you for good."

"You needed somebody to take care of you, didn't you?" She broke off a large chunk of a roll and stuffed it in her mouth, staring down at her plate.

Denver watched the two in their misery, pulling some joy away from the others. Would be nice if William and his family were here, he thought. He had always regretted that William's family had stayed in California, though they had certainly visited often, and stayed in touch. Why, there was an e-mail message from one of them every day or so. He thought that William, and then Ronald, ought to be on the farm. It was in their blood. Probably that was what had drawn Ronald to the environmental cause. Funny, how his parents had been part of a generation that swept across the west, appropriating land and resources as needed for their livelihood and their great-grandson was part of a movement that said, "Whoa, wait a minute. Don't use it all up!"

And Sarah—he always thought of her as little Sarah, even when she grew up, received her MBA at Berkeley, lived in San Francisco, and had an executive position with a computer company.

William had, after years of struggle, left the corporate world and bought a franchise print shop that was near his home.

"Never been happier. Susan works with me and we seem to work all the time, but it's together, so that's all right. I haven't missed that commute one day. Do you realize how much time you gain by not spending an hour or two going to work each day?"

When the pair traveled with Elizabeth and Daniel to Europe two years before, they had invited Denver and Noreen to go, but Denver had declined. Noreen was openly disappointed. Perhaps she would go after he died, with a group from the retirement center. He knew the small world that his wife, Emma, had lived in was tiny compared to many of the next generation, and he lived somewhere between the two. Never really figuring out computers because, why would he? Using what gadgets were simple in his hand, taking what medical examinations that he needed with the fancy new machines, but letting much of the high-tech age slip past him as something that had arrived too late to be relevant to him.

He felt a little foreign to much of the talk that drift-ed around him, as if a new age had come, and he was not a participant. Noreen went to the computer room and sent e-mail messages. Sometimes he went along, but he preferred, really, to talk about the old days. He was drifting, he thought, on a float, disconnected from megabytes, hardware, and electronic wizardry, and somehow even the connections to his children loosened or were kept in place by ties from yesterday more than hopes for tomorrow.

He was slowing down, losing his appetite for life and food. He thought about death frequently and of how his passing would be for Noreen. He thought she would be okay — good that they were here where she knew people. She was self-sufficient. He had wanted to fling Bobbie's words back at him. Noreen had grown up with stingy parents and limited education but...did Aunt Hilda make the difference? Bobbie had caring people in his life...what was it made some crops thrive and others shrivel? "You could have made something of your life after you came back from Vietnam! We all tried to help you," Denver wanted to say to Bobbie, but Bobbie would have taken this as reinforcement for the failure of his life, would have said, "And even with your help, I've come to noth-in'."

Martha told Benjy she had to go home, so Benjy took her and Bobbie. The rest of the family was still visiting when Benjy returned and Denver could see his grandson move gladly into conversations, relieved to be with the rest of the family.

It was late when Sally, Noreen, and Denver returned to the car. The night was clear and filled with stars as the car glided along the lane. He caught a glimpse of a sturdy, well-built fence on his side of the lane, across from the lane of tall trees, and was glad.

The next morning, Denver, Noreen, and Sally walked to the dining room together, stopping on the way to admire one of Alice's paintings. Denver and Noreen greeted other residents, pausing at a few tables to introduce Sally. The residents noticed and took interest in any strangers who came to a meal.

"I hear you're a Congress...m...woman." This from a frail-looking woman wrapped in a lavender wool shawl, with oxygen tubes attached to the bottom of her nose. She reached her hand toward Sally. Sally took the bony hand. The woman's white hair was thin, the pink scalp beneath it visible. "Well, I congratulate you. Always said things would be better when women had a hand in what's goin' on."

"I agree with you. We don't have enough women yet, but at least...it's better than it used to be."

People at other tables stared openly. Probably they would all like to meet Sally personally, but that was not what she was there for, so Denver ignored the interest and led her to an empty table.

While most signs of pretense were gone in the seniors—no one bragged about what he or she was going to do—they were not beyond being impressed. Just last week, Denver had said to a couple of people, "My granddaughter, the Congresswoman from California, is coming to visit."

Noreen had smiled fondly at him when he said this, though she never mentioned Sally's position to anyone. Just now, Noreen had stopped to speak with a bridge partner. Denver took the opportunity to speak about Noreen to Sally: "To know her is to know her completely—all the way through. There is nothing in her that is secretive, or conniving, or devious."

"Yes," Sally agreed. "She also has a kind heart. When Bryce died, Elizabeth and I were over the edge with grief. We all were. Noreen sat with us, cried with us. She never made those speeches like, 'Well it's time to get on with your life,' or 'God had a purpose in this.' She didn't say we should be proud because he died for his country. Oh, I'm sure she prayed, but she didn't preach at us."

"When I first met her, I was cut up with losing Emma. Didn't know what to do next. She didn't tell me to get over it. She just helped me take a step at a time. And, I guess when you do that, new things come along. New challenges. So, inevitably, you do move on, but that doesn't minimize the loss."

"You are a very lucky man—to have had two good women."

"Yes. I wonder...Mrs. Maloney isn't at breakfast. Excuse me." He spoke to someone at the next table. "Is Iris Maloney doing okay?"

"Hasn't been feelin' too well lately. She's on the other side."

"Oh. Goodness. I hope she's okay."

"Never can tell when you will go over there."

"The other side is the other wing, where you go when you need more care. If you can't get out of bed or take care of yourself. It's more like a hospital," Denver explained.

Noreen sat down. "Yes. It's one of the reasons we came here. They have all levels of care. That old gentleman over there — his wife has Alzheimer disease. She lives on the other side. He goes over every day to see her. Sometimes he brings her over here in a wheelchair."

"We're glad the other side is there, still, but we're all a little anxious about goin' over there." This was coming home to Denver, as he felt himself slowing down. What would that be…to not be? If he were lucky, he would die in his sleep, not have the rush of uniformed people, the terror of emergency rooms. "You got a lot longer to live it and enjoy it than I did," he heard Emma say. He thought of her occasionally now, and sometimes memories of her blended with those of Noreen, so he could not remember which one he was with when Sally was born or little Sarah came from California the first time with William and Susan. Course, he could figure it out when he stopped to do so. Emma died in '56, Sally knew her, while little Sarah was born later, in '58, he thought. Still, in idle moments, when his mind turned to the past, perhaps because there was so little future to turn to, the past blurred. His parents were almost mythical, yet lately the memories of them had been heightened.

He would not see Alice's children become adults. He might not live to see Victoria mature enough to remove from her appearance the flaming announcements of her independence. He rather liked her dress, anyway. She might be a creature from Mars, an alien that they talk about now. He had watched her at the computer terminal, green hair, purple vest, jewelry hanging everywhere, amongst the pale, gray, residents, and he thought of yellow daffodils popping out of the ground in their brightness.

"Granddad," she said one day, "You know Mr. Brown? Did you know he was a judge for thirty years? And Mrs. Sanders raised seven children and taught piano lessons all through the years?"

"She plays very well. Sometimes she performs for us. Never heard anybody do 'Twelfth Street Rag' better."

"And the lady with the oxygen...she's lived all over the world."

Then, as had happened at the dinner last night, the faces around him became impressionistic and those of his parents and siblings had blended in front of him. He was circling back to where it all started. He had heard that the oldest memories were the last to go. A fear rose in him that he was walking into a wall that he could not see.

"I'm going out to visit Martha and Bobbie a little later." Then, as if Sally had read his thoughts, "You know what I would like to do later today? If it's all right with you — set up a recorder and ask you both some questions about the early days in your lives."

"Well, dunno there's much you don't already know, but we can try. This is what happens when folks see the end nearing."

"Oh, I'm sorry," Sally said.

"No reason to be," Denver responded. "Better to accept than deny."

"Forget the recorder. We'll just visit," Sally decided.

"Still, you being a historian and all, accuracy is important. I should pull out some pictures and old records." Noreen was looking thoughtful. "I'll do that. It'll be fun."

"The recorder is fine. If you are going to be quoting me when I'm not here to defend myself, then better to have it recorded," Denver smiled fondly at Sally.

"I'd like to know more about my grandmother's early life and family. Since she had no brothers or sisters and her parents died when she was a child, I've had no contact with her family. Have you?"

"Not much." He sipped his coffee thoughtfully. "Seems to me at the time of her death, a couple of cousins showed up, but that's 'bout all…let me think about it."

"I've started working on genealogy," Noreen said, "Another thing lots of old folks do, you know. The Mormons send someone over one day a week to work with us."

"Great! And you are working on…?"

"Mostly Denver's family because, like Emma, I have no siblings. So, I have charts going on your family, both sides and my own. Very interesting."

"You are somewhat of a historian yourself."

"Well, you know, like you, Sally, I have no offspring of my own. Your family is mine, but no one carries my genetic code into another generation."

"Maybe we should clone ourselves."

"I think you should. At least you have brothers. I don't. Funny how, as you get on in age, you think about those things. Maybe it means something to see your name on a chart, like you were a link in the chain of humanity. I guess no one wants her name erased from a chalkboard as if she never existed."

"'Course Sally will go down in the history books — not just the ones she writes. We just don't know yet how large. Maybe she'll be president one day."

"Or pursue an honorable career." Sally's companions nodded, understanding the reference to the recent sex scandal that had engulfed the White House.

He liked the silences and the comfort among the three of them, and that Sally was here. It was like… but that was it…this comparing everything to something past. All the signposts were behind him. This might be the last time he would see Sally. A part of him wanted to make time stand still, while another part relished this visit but could let it go, let everything go…like he had the farm. He had stood there that day when the moving van came, and young men were loading furniture that would go with them. He hadn't been able to take his eyes off the land, the line of trees along the lane, the mountains. The landscape of his life. He was always a little startled to look outside and see the freeway and tall buildings.

Still, that was the key, letting everything go, and though he had never been, in modern terms, "a control freak," he found leaving the farm difficult, as well as accepting his own death.

"It's the quality of the life we live while we're here that's important. How much joy, caring, knowledge, and challenge we have. How many daisies we picked and did we enjoy the picking. How much we laughed. How much we held one another." Noreen looked toward Sally and Denver, who seemed absorbed in thought.

"Noreen, this is very personal, but your faith has always been personal for you. I don't know anyone who practices Christianity more and preaches it less. Where does that strength come from? I don't think your parents taught you, from what you've said," Sally remarked.

"No, but my aunt—my friend, really—took me to church with her," Noreen commented. "My parents didn't care because it got me out of their hair for a couple of hours. I'm not sure I can explain it…I guess that's what faith is…'the substance of things hoped for, the evidence of things not seen.' And I don't think it can ever be entirely explained."

"Do you believe in heaven and hell?" Sally asked.

"I know what the church teaches. I'm not a theologian. I've never been able to take a narrow interpretation of which person God's favor falls upon. I don't believe in eternal damnation—not from the Bible or my own mind. There is a scripture that says, 'In the fullness of time, He will unite all things in one, even in Him.' I love that thought. It seems so right. I just don't see any point in burning people forever. I'm more forgiving than that, so surely God is."

"And quite possibly, the definition of 'forever' has changed since ancient times. We all use that term metaphorically—'I thought I was stuck in that Denver Airport forever,' when the time was a few hours," Sally smiled.

Noreen continued: "Right. You know. When you've made the circuit from childhood to old age, I think you see that, when people do evil, probably someone did evil to them. In other words, there is cause and effect, which does not remove our responsibility for what we do, but it may—in my mind it does—make hell an unreasonable penalty. I just can't buy it—it's more Catholic theology than anything else.

"We don't think so much in terms of sin these days, but when I grew up, we heard lots about sin. I used to think I was going to burn in hell because I certainly sinned 'in word, thought or deed' regularly. I used to worry about it. Some people in the church would say not to trust your own reasoning, just believe what they tell you. Well, I could never do that. After all, God gave me the ability to reason."

"When I was a kid," Denver began, "we didn't question our parents, the church, any authority, and I must admit, I've never got used to the way young folks question everything, even though I know sometimes, they're right."

He continued: "Sally, now, you asked me about heaven, and I want to say, I don't know. I know what works. I talk to God. I tell Him my concerns and my joys. I read the Bible. I sing the hymns. I feel at peace, at rest in my soul. I feel watched over, protected, and loved. And, that's enough, I'm okay with whatever happens after I die."

"That's wonderful. So you two are comfortable with this business of dying?" Sally asked.

"Well," Denver said roughly, "it's not exactly something to look forward to. I worry about pain or losing my marbles."

"As far as pain, you should not have to worry about that. Have you written instructions? There's no cause to be heroic," Sally said.

"Yes."

"Actually, I believe that Alzheimer's would have already occurred if it was going to. As far as dementia…I don't know."

"They monitor us here and we both do the things we can to be healthy, watch our cholesterol, and so forth. We have each other and the family who care about us."

"I guess that is as close as you get to a guarantee."

Noreen crunched on a piece of toast. "I was thinking about Victoria. Seems like, the new always has to challenge the old. Whether it is Victoria, or you, Sally, or young Ronald. An environmentalist—your folks, Denver, wouldn't even know what that meant."

"They were in the wave that came west, took the land, and worked it so they could live," Denver shook his head. "So much change. You get to the place; you don't want to adapt anymore. You don't want to think about it."

"Course we're glad for medical technology — the by-pass you had a few years ago, dear. Our generation went from the horse-and-buggy era to space travel and the Internet. How much can anyone take in?" Noreen asked.

When Sally left around eleven o'clock, Denver and Noreen were poring through memorabilia, rekindling their memories. In addition to Bobbie and Martha, Sally planned to stop by to see Alice's studio. It was nearly four o'clock when she returned. Somewhere along the way, she had lost some of the calmness that had been with her when she left.

She had gone to Alice's first, and described the studio as "marvelous chaos…and the light…I wanted to stay. I wish I could say something good about Mother's. A visiting nurse was there when I arrived, helping Mother bathe, so I had a chance to visit with Bobbie, but I think he was stoned."

"He's definitely dependent on the drugs he takes," Noreen said.

"If he'd only gotten out of there after he came back from Vietnam," Denver said. "He tried. Michele helped him get into an apartment, but Martha resisted all the way."

Denver had never forgotten the look Martha gave Michele when Bobbie brought her to a family dinner — the first time most of the family had met her. Martha had looked up when the couple entered, taking in the arms entwined, the broad smile on Michele's face.

"This is my mother, Martha, Martha Samuels," Bobbie had said, pleading silently, "Don't go off!"

She had not. She just sat staring at the young woman, her body turning to stone as she looked, her eyes becoming cold, and the jawline rigid. She had clamped her mouth shut. "I see."

Marianne, engaged to marry Benjy, had stepped in then, welcoming Michele, asking about her work, her children. Martha said little, eating voraciously, angrily slopping the food down.

After Michele and Bobbie left, Benjy had tried to dispel some of the tension evident in his mother. "So what do you think, Ma?"

"Well, we'll see about this. I'll not have that woman in my house."

"Why not, Ma? Don't you want Bobbie to have his own life? Why, he's only twenty-five. He's got a lot of life ahead of him and your life will be easier once he's on his own."

"So you think you got it all figured out, huh? Well, we'll just see about that."

"Martha, I hope you'll give Michele a chance,"

Denver had said. "Bobbie needs this, you know. He's too young to be old."

"And she's got children already! She's lookin' for a built-in daddy! Don't you know she's got her eyes on her needs, not his?"

"That may be true, Martha. Still, in all fairness, not every young woman is going to look adoringly at Bobbie. She knows what his problems are and…"

"I'll have no more talk of this!" Martha had thundered. "I know what's best for Bobbie. And that's final!"

Driving home that night, in 1973, Denver and Noreen were quiet. Martha's attitude shocked and frightened them.

When Martha saw that even her fury would not end the relationship between Bobbie and Michele, and they began to talk of marriage, she suggested that after the honeymoon they move in with her so they could save money to buy a house. Michele had two children: a boy, five years old, and a girl seven.

"Martha," Denver had asked, "Have you thought about this? Do you really want that whole family living with you?"

"I'm just tryin' to help out. I'm just thinkin' of them. Course it won't be easy for me."

Still she had persisted, appealing to the business side of Michele, showing her on paper how much sooner they could have their own home if they lived, rent free, with her.

Finally, Bobbie and Michele agreed. It hadn't gone well. Martha had wanted Bobbie there, and tolerated

Michele and her children, reminding them constantly
of how much she was giving them by providing a
home. Denver and Noreen had heard Martha turn
herself into a martyr, "for Bobbie and those folks."

She had fixed meals for Bobbie and herself.
Michele had to fix a separate meal for herself and the
children, with Martha saying, "Don't use that pan,"
and "That's my butter," yelling it at the children, who
scurried about quietly trying to avoid Martha, wide-
eyed and afraid.

"It's me or your mother," Michele had finally said
to Bobbie, "I can't live here when she hates me and
my children. I'm moving out. Are you coming or
not?"

"Y…yes, but let me talk to her." He had spoken to
his mother. She had softened her criticism for a few
days. Then the boy had broken a vase that had belonged to Emma, Martha's mother. It sat on a coffee
table near where the children played. When it fell,
shattering beyond repair, Martha's arm swept out and
knocked the child down. Bobbie sat frozen. He had
never seen his mother strike anyone. Michele hadn't
been home at the time and Bobbie had gone to the
boy to soothe him.

"Sympathizing with him! She's turnin' you against
me!"

"The child is more important than the vase, Mother." Bobbie continued to try to make peace between
his mother and his wife, but by that time, Michele had
rented a small house. When she learned that her son
had been hit, she packed the children off to a friend's

house for the remaining days before she could move into the house.

"Are you comin' or not?"

"Yeah, but…maybe it's best if you move out first. Then Mom will simmer down and I'll come, too."

"She's never going to let you go. Don't you see that? She'll keep you with guilt or anger or whatever it takes. Well, you know where to find me."

As soon as Michele left, Martha had had the ramp built so it was easy for Bobbie to go in and out of the house in his wheelchair. She encouraged him to do that rather than walk, so he wouldn't get "too tired."

He had gone to visit Michele and stayed all night a few times. When he did, Martha called about once every hour. "This meat loaf is going to spoil unless you come home to eat it! I made it for you!" An hour later, she called, "Where's that blue towel I always use for my hair?" Then, "I found your pills. How are you going to get on all night without your pills?"

Michele had the telephone number changed and unlisted. Martha had driven to the house, not coming inside, but sitting in the car honking the horn until Bobbie emerged, hearing her screaming questions and anger at him like a wild woman. To appease her, he would go home. Eventually, Michele tired of this.

Noreen had run into Michele at the grocery store one day during this period. She was brusque with Noreen, and the older woman had the feeling she would have dodged her entirely, sweeping furiously down a different aisle, but the two women approached each other, neither seeing the other until their carts nearly hit.

Michele's hair had been uncombed. She wore no makeup. A large, dirty pink top covered her Levis to mid-thigh. She wore sandals. Her toenails and finger-nails were painted, but the red coloring had chipped away. Her eyes flashed. Her face was unsmiling and set. Her elbows jutted out on either side of the cart as if to confront anything in her path.

"Hello, Michele. How are you?"

"You should ask." She bent over to pick up a bag of chocolate chip cookies. "Somebody should have warned me. What am I to do with that worthless Momma's boy that is my husband? Spineless as a wet noodle!"

"I'm sorry, Michele. I know…"

"Lot of good that does me!"

Noreen had said nothing.

Michele's shoulders had dropped a little from the arched position. Her voice grew quieter but was still angry. "Oh, I know it's not your fault, and everyone tells me I should have seen it coming. I thought he would change, but, that woman…she has a hold on him and, by god, she's not going to let go."

"I'm afraid you're right, Michele. We've talked to her, but on some things…she gets that determined look and we know she's not hearing us."

"I never had a chance with her." The words had come out dully. "But I thought I had a chance with him." Noreen saw that the younger woman was angry with herself for having made a bad choice. "Two failed marriages and I'm not even thirty!"

"Michele. I had a failed marriage before I married Denver, so don't you go thinking that you're a failure. You have two children, very nice ones, I think. You've done well at your job. You really care about those kids. It shows in the way that you handle them. That's really important."

Michele had brushed something away from her eyes. "Yes, I suppose you're right. Thank you. I didn't really want to see you, but I'm glad I did."

"Now, listen to me. You're welcome at our home any time. No matter what happens between you and Bobbie or Martha. When those blues start getting to you, you call me up and come on out. There's too much good in you to waste on thinking about being a failure. You hear me now?"

Noreen had come home from the store that day in 1977 and told Denver about Michele. The pair had invited her out, had taken care of the children, listened to the young woman talk about her job, the children's school, or whatever she wanted to talk about.

Bobbie's life had plunged into free fall with the end of his second marriage. Michele had plugged along, holding job and children and life together with all she could muster and with added strength from Noreen and Denver's support. Calling them one day, she said, "I got a promotion! I want to celebrate. Can I take you two out to dinner — and bring the kids?"

They'd met her and the children at an all-you-can-eat diner. The children had been scrubbed and clean.

Michele was too. They had chattered away, talking about work, school, and a soccer team.

"I'm so proud of you," Noreen had said.

Michele had eventually remarried when the children were in college. Gradually the contact with her had diminished, though they still exchanged Christmas cards.

"You'll never know…how much you helped me." Michele told Noreen. She called later about plans for getting married again. "You made such a difference. You gave me backbone and belief in myself when I needed it."

Staying at his mother's house after Michele left, Bobbie found little reason to get up in the morning. He hated going to the bank—seeing Michele—he told his grandfather. Frequent absences and inattention to the details of the job eventually brought about his dismissal. By 1978, the divorce was final.

When Bobbie lost his job at the bank, he took other positions, but none lasted long. He tumbled into an abyss of despair, and beyond into a dull land without sharpness of image or brightness of color. He watched television most of the day, occasionally driving the motorized wheelchair Martha had bought for him a block or two to buy fast food or candy or cheap beer.

Sometimes, he hung about there, talking with some of the regulars, watching people come and go. Life slid by him one day at a time, and though he thought sometimes to slow the tide, he mostly just let it go.

Sitting in the living room of Denver and Noreen's apartment, Sally's mind was on Bobbie, unable to free itself from the depression and misery in which her mother and brother lived.

"She was a good mother to me. Sometimes I don't even recognize who she has become."

"I suppose we've seen it happening on a day-to-day basis for a long time, so it isn't such a shock. She was a good mother, but her self-esteem was never high. Her job made that better. She was doing okay just before Bobbie came home; still, the divorce was hard on her self-confidence. She really hung on to Bobbie."

"She never thought men would be interested in her. She was surprised when Benjamin was. She compared herself unfavorably to Elizabeth," Denver said.

"Whatever happened, the gloom has settled there so heavy it is almost unbearable. I offered to pay to have someone come in and clean weekly, but she says, 'I'll have no strangers in the house.' She's afraid of everything. A break-in occurred at a neighbor's house, so she's become completely paranoid. I counted seven locks on the front door."

"Lots of people are afraid anymore. There have even been break-ins here."

"Oh, really? I don't know how to help either of them. You know, I go away. I get involved in other things. It's easy to forget, but it isn't. I don't want to forget them. I care, but I don't know how to make a difference," Sally mused.

"We feel the same way. I send e-mail messages to Bobbie, but he rarely responds," Noreen said.

"I thought when I sent the computer, it would get him away from watching so much television. But it's just another way to waste time. He plays Solitaire on it or goes into chat rooms and talks with other people like himself—lonely, separated from the world," Sally remarked.

"It is such a relief to see the rest of the family. Benjy and Marianne, oh, I know they have some problems with Dennie. No one is without problems, but they're enthusiastic about life. They love the old place. Who'd have thought Benjy would be the one to end up living there? Grandad, have you thought anymore about my grandmother's family?" She went into the bedroom, brought out a small tape recorder, and placed it on the table. "Just forget it's there."

"We pulled out what we have. She was raised by her Aunt Bertha."

On the table in front of them was a small pile of old photographs, letters, and papers. Sally began picking each one up, scrutinizing it, and listening as Denver told what he could about each item.

"Emma lived with her Aunt Bertha when I met her. They lived in a tiny cottage near downtown. No bigger than a minute—a kitchen and bedroom was all there was to it. The two shared the bed. Bertha was very quiet, a kind of private woman, you know. In those days, everybody didn't talk about their problems like they do nowadays."

"We grew up hearing, 'You don't air your dirty linen in public.' People do now. They get on talk shows and tell amazingly personal stories," Noreen added.

Sally smiled.

Denver continued: "Anyway, Emma never talked about her parents. She didn't know what happened to them. When I was commencing to marry her, on our wedding day, it was, Bertha sat me down and said, 'Now you know, she's got no family but me. I've never told her…her parents died in a fire when she was a baby. A miracle she got out…a neighbor walked out of the building holding this bundle. Everybody crowded around afraid she might be dead, too, but she cried then, and they looked down at a baby whose parents were dead, and I suppose they wondered what life held for this child. I was cookin' 'bout ten miles away for the miners. Someone got word to me. Since I was the only known livin' relative, I took her.'"

That conversation came clear to Denver. That warm afternoon in the garden—swatches of color stuck in his mind, of gold, pink, red, and the puffy white clouds in a blue sky. The wedding had been at the church. After the wedding his family and a few neighbors who were there hitched up the horses, piled in the wagons, and drove to Bertha's place for cake and punch in the garden.

Days ahead, Bertha had clipped dead flowers, pulled weeds, and mowed the grass, so everything that day was fresh as a newborn.

Bertha's hair was a mixture of dark brown and gray, pulled back in a bun that nestled against her neck. Usually, she wore a shapeless thin cotton house-dress in a flowered print with an apron that covered her entire front. On his wedding day she wore a beautiful blue dress that gathered at the waist, and he saw her figure outlined in it and realized that his image of a formless lump beneath the everyday clothes was wrong. Vivacious and lovely, that's when Bertha had taken him aside to tell him about Emma's history.

The hydrangeas, marigolds, petunias, and gardenias bloomed around them. The roses grew along the fence. And he so full of love for Emma and the idea that she would have him. What did he care where she came from? It was where she was going that interested him. He listened politely to Bertha, thinking of holding Emma, very close. Noticing his attention wander, Bertha had laid a hand on his knee.

"I listened to her, but my head was in the clouds that day. Bertha told me, 'Her father was my brother. When he and his wife died in the fire, I wrote to our parents back in Iowa. They sent me a little money. With what her parents had saved, I bought this property, and folks helped me build the cottage. Just big enough for the two of us.'"

"What ever happened to Great Aunt Bertha?"

"Not long after we were married, one of her parents—her mother, I think, took sick back in Iowa; they wanted Bertha to help take care of her, so she sold the property and went east. It was hard for Emma to see her go—she knew she might never see her again. She never did. No telephones, 'course. Emma was having babies and taking care of my parents. They wrote, but over the years, came to be more and more time between letters. Sort of lost touch, I guess, and never made it up. A few times over the years, we heard somethin'…Noreen found a couple of letters, didn't you?"

"Yes, but first," Noreen picked up a picture and handed it to Sally. "We think these are Emma's parents. And below the picture, see where the writing's nearly faded? I think it says, 'Harold and Willa Hailey.' That would be her parents. This other one isn't noted at all, but I think, see—this man—isn't that the same person? Probably Harold's family."

"My great grandparents. Isn't it funny how we look for something that connects us and all we have are a couple of photographs. When this generation leaves, it will be with a trail of videotapes, albums, cards, but not many letters. It's too bad that Aunt Bertha faded out of your life and along with her that whole part of our history. One of these days, after I am through in Congress, I'll go back and look into all this."

"Hardly time for you to be talkin' about being through. You just started," Denver said.

"Yes. I'm pulled in two directions. I like research and writing about history. But I think there's some necessary work to be done in Congress, too."

"You're lucky to have such opportunities, and the country is fortunate to have you. Here's a picture at the wedding. In the garden. This is Aunt Bertha." Noreen picked up a black-edged envelope, took out the card inside. "This is the notice of her death."

Denver took the card and held it. "She died in 1932. Only forty-two. 'Course, people didn't live as long then. It's a shame though—she's practically forgotten—none of my children knew her and she never had any of her own. Still, she raised Emma. She taught her how to tend the earth, to cook and can. She made Emma what she was, much more than her parents did."

"I think there were many Aunt Berthas, who cooked and cleaned and cared for other people; but because they were childless and not married, they are almost forgotten," Sally suggested.

"Like my Aunt Hilda," Noreen said.

"Yes. Now that you mention it, Sally, hope I'm not too personal, but do you ever regret not having children?"

"Sometimes I do."

"But you'll be remembered for other things. I feel like Denver's children are mine; still genetically they're not."

"I'm not so sure that being replicated genetically is all that important. You've shared our lives for over

forty years now. I don't know that we would have made it after Bryce died without your steadiness.
I was five when my grandmother died. I have this fuzzy memory of her, but I've known you all these years. Do you remember my grandmother?"

"Yes." Noreen smiled. "She was beautiful. I remember her auburn hair and her cheekbones, high and proud, and her large, wide-set eyes. Well, I never really knew her. We said hello when she came into the diner, but she didn't pay me much mind. Why would she?"

Denver slipped away from the two women. In his mind, he liked going back. Noreen's description of Emma brought her back to him, and he felt a longing for his youth and passion. How she opened herself to him so completely was the miracle of his life—and Noreen another, softer miracle. Emma. Nothing could replace that first exploration of her woman's body. It was not really that he wanted children: he wanted her. He would have endured almost anything for that pleasure.

"My father," Denver told Sally, "lost property several times before settling on the place in Kuna. He would have gone on selling and moving, but my mother refused to go again."

"That would be understandable. All the kids—ten that grew up. I don't know how she did it."

"I remember my mother sayin', 'There's nothin' worse than gettin' into that wagon with everything you own and no place to put it. Nowhere to go. They call us settlers, well it's time we settled."

"Did you ever think of selling and moving on?"

"Many times." The anxiety of farming came back to him. He could feel the muscles in his stomach pull tight. Were the cattle safe and well? Would the corn grow without disease or weather damage? Would the price fall before he was able to get the product to market? Would the children be fed? The taxes and the lien on the property satisfied? "But, you see, it was the early '30s when my folks died. The country was in a depression. Me, with no education, so manual labor was all I could get, and there were dozens standing around for every job available."

"It's hard to believe, Sally, in these days of the proliferation of stuff, how little people had back then. To get an orange at Christmas was a big deal. Or a lump of coal. Now people have so much."

"Everyone doesn't. We have many homeless in San Francisco. Still, I agree, most people have and are accumulating lots of stuff."

"Now, not many people go to war. Instead, they have big homes and many possessions. Are people happier, more content?" Noreen asked.

"Don't think so. Never realized when we were struggling to make a go of it on the farm that people would look back and call those times the good old days." Denver remarked. "What do you think, Sally?"

"Such a big question. Some things have changed for the better. I see bumper stickers calling for 'random acts of kindness,' but it's the random acts of violence that come into every home through television and somehow enter our psyche, leaving us feeling frightened and unsafe," Sally replied.

Noreen added, "Many lives are easier than their parents' and grandparents', but because we only relate to our own experience, we really don't understand how much better, more convenient, simpler things are. It's all taken for granted. So, are people happier with all this new wealth?"

"I don't know how to answer that on a broad basis. Look at our family. Most of us are leading good, productive lives. We don't get up every morning and say, I'm happy. One tends to notice when one is unhappy. And, there is Bobbie and Mother — definitely unhappy," Sally responded.

Denver said, "I was thinkin' about my father. I don't know that he was happy…certainly, he was not content. I remember when someone offered him a good price for the land. He told my mother. She just stood there at the stove where it seemed she always was. Didn't say anything…didn't have to. The interested party came by the next day, with an agreement for signature. Father was in the field at the time. Seeing the man's horse and buggy, he dropped what he was doing and made for the house. He got there in time to hear Mother say, 'It's not for sale.' She spit those words out like she had tasted something bitter."

"And your father didn't argue?" Noreen asked.

"No...I never understood that. He ruled the family with an iron hand, but when mother put her foot down, well that was it," Denver said.

"Marriage, too has changed. In the good ones it's more of a partnership," Sally added.

"I watched my father dominate with bluster and cuffings and preachings about God, but he always wanted more money. Mother didn't preach, but she lived a more merciful Christianity and was more practical in mundane matters. I s'pose my father knew that, though he would never have acknowledged it."

Perhaps his father wanted her warmth, not anger, flowing toward him. Women often brought a grace or kindness to life that men needed, without which life was hollow and meaningless. It was the whole of the woman, not her body alone, that satisfied and fulfilled, but all the softness, goodness, and forbearance she contained.

Then Denver thought of Emma. She had come to the barn one day when no one else was around, wanting to tell him something. He had pulled her down on the straw, lifting her skirts, entering her. Then, she was picking the straw from her hair and clothes when he came up from behind and grasped her breasts in his hands, and pushed himself into her again, never having enough of her.

Aw-w, life. He was an old man now and not that for long.

Sally brought Bobbie in to Denver and Noreen's place the next day, hoping that she might find some way, some key, with which to help him.

The four of them walked to the dining room together around noon. Bobbie, who could have dated any girl in high school, with his dark wavy hair, football muscles, and confident air, now was the frailest among them. His hair was long and uncombed. His clothes and posture were sloppy. The sunken eyes looked down mostly or not far ahead. His flesh was yellow, and his hands shaky. Next to the healthy exuberance of Sally, he was startling. Other residents looked and then looked away.

After they sat down and began eating, Sally said, "I hate seeing you and mother sick and unhappy, but I don't know how to help you. Tell me how, Bobbie."

Bobbie looked at her, glanced away, staring down at his food. A tear showed in his eye.

"I don't know, Sister. I know you want to help me, but nothin' 'cept what I'm doin' seems possible now."

"Do you go to any of the Veterans Groups?"

"No. I used to, but got tired of it. Those guys sitting around complaining 'bout the government. How it ought to do more for them."

"Do you think the government does enough, then?"

Bobbie looked down at the vegetable soup in front of him. He hardly touched his food. He stared away from the table for a while, then answered, "Well, it's hard to say. It's like, you know, I watch these talk shows on television and people come on who have had someone close to them murdered, and they want the death penalty for the murderer, want to watch him die, as if that will square things. The government ordered us to this war in Vietnam. Was that right? Well, you can say better than I can, but what happened there can't be squared. The government can't give me enough money to get my real arm and leg back, or to give me back what else I lost there."

"You still have life, Bobbie."

"But not hope. Oh, I tried. Here I was, one year, playin' football and chasin' girls, and the next, fightin' a war."

"Did you think you would go on playing football and chasing girls forever?"

"Didn't think much about it, but don't you see, I had no idea, really, of what my life would be. If I'd made it with Debbie or Michele…"

"How about Victoria? You could still have a relationship with your daughter."

"Could I? She never comes over anymore, or calls."

"She sends e-mail. Do you answer her?"

"Oh, yeah, that, well, that's just e-mail. I read it."

"Seems like your grandmother is more up-to-date than you are."

"Just don't bother with it."

"What do you bother with, Bobbie? What do you want?"

"I guess, I guess…I guess, nothin'. Seems for a long time that there was so much distance between what I wanted and what was possible, I guess I stopped bothering to want."

"I don't even know how to respond." Sally's voice was low and plaintive. "I can't…"

"Can't imagine being where I am? Sister, the distance between where you are and I am is like the miles between want and reality. I can't imagine your life and you can't believe mine."

"I want to bridge that gap, Bobbie. I want something more for the rest of your life."

"But I'm not sure I do." His words came out slow as if he were writing the letters, pecking at an old typewriter, in his mind. "I guess I've given up. I could say something else, to make you feel better. I could make a plan with you and you would go away hopeful, but life has beaten me. It wasn't entirely what happened in Vietnam. It was mother. She wanted to take care of me. She needed that, and I knew, somewhere, that it wasn't going to be good for me in the long run, but after awhile, I guess, I just let it happen. She wanted me to be there more than I didn't want it. I don't care anymore.

"It was the drugs, which make it too easy, and it was me — my weakness, my inability to take myself in hand with enough determination to make things better. Maybe you got a gene I didn't, Sally. Every family has its successes and its failures. I played a role."

Silence took the table then, as if no words existed in the language or in the universe that would mitigate or change Bobbie's life or the distance between these two siblings.

Denver thought of Martha, at home, weary of existence. He felt young next to his daughter and grandson. Still, he felt old because of them.

"My soaps come on soon. Can I watch them here?"

Early the next morning, Elizabeth came to take Sally to the airport. The two took easy pleasure and comfort in each other's presence.

"Sally ought to have been Elizabeth's daughter," Denver said to Noreen once. "It isn't just that they look alike."

"It's a melding of spirit and mind, of intellect and instinct. Wonderful women you produced, my dear."

"And what of Martha?"

"She is more troubling."

"Parents want to love all their children the same, and they try to be fair. Still I must admit, Elizabeth was easier to love than Martha. From the beginning. I can't say why and I've never admitted that before."

"Do you think Emma felt that way, too?"

"Can't say. We never talked about it." He saw the two little girls standing together in new, light and fluffy — was it organza? — dresses Emma had made them for Easter. Martha frowning, pulling at her sister's hand. Elizabeth smiling.

Chapter Twelve

Bobbie's fax continued:

"The frequent feelings of suicide have been running rampant in my mind and I know this is disappointing to you and you'll hate me for this but the release is what I need for my mind to be free of worry and black thoughts because it feels so bad to sit with someone trying to have a good time and knowing that you are just going through the motions. I can only put on so many false smiles and fake it for so long."

Denver and Noreen celebrated Christmas, 1997, at Benjy's house with the rest of the family. Everyone, especially the children, hoped for a white Christmas, for big flakes to pelt downward, rest in the trees.

"Oh, the parks in Boise—Julia Davis and Ann Morrison—when the snow clings in the trees, when it freezes so the branches grow heavy and white," Noreen said. "It's so beautiful. I love it."

This year, however, no snow had fallen. The dull brown earth lay barren. The trees stood stark and skeletal. Nor did the overcast gray sky offer any color to break the monotonous landscape in this, the darkest and heaviest time of the year.

Still Elizabeth and Daniel, Alice and Hau Soun and the children, Maria and Steven, Victoria, Benjy, and Marianne, and their two children who were home, Jody and Jolanda, along with Denver and Noreen, created warmth against the chill that Martha and Bobbie carried with them.

"Oh, I'm glad you brought your guitar, Dad," Victoria said. "I brought mine, so we can play together. Let's go in the other room and practice."

Denver watched the two figures leaving the room. Victoria, bouncy and bright, her life ahead of her and so full of opportunities. She was out of the room and picking at her guitar before Bobbie had finished his shuffling exit.

Later, after dinner, the two sat together with their guitars, strumming as the voices of the family sang, "Silent Night, Holy Night," "Joy To The World," and other familiar carols. Martha sat sleeping in her wheelchair, her breathing uneven and noisy.

"I didn't want the singing to stop," Denver said later to Noreen, "I didn't want this day to end."

"I know. I felt it too, as if the singing was holding back something awful."

"What was the fax, Grandad?" Benjy asked coming down the hall. Wordlessly, Denver handed it to him.

"Oh, Jesus, you guys, I've never felt so completely disconnected from anything normal in such a long time and the weakness both mental and physical is just torture. Please, if you can somewhere in your heart find a place for me and forgive me for any and all pain and suffering I may have caused you then that would be so greatly appreciated. God only knows how all this has come about and what has fueled my manic disorder and why these things are so very hard for me to deal with now. I have not done well though my heart I think was in the right place. I want for you nothing but the best. Please get over this and understand that I will be at rest which is the thing that I need most at this time. I am exhausted and battered beyond repair so I must go."

The fax had rung also at Sally's home. She heard the sound, but did not respond. (Other telephone calls came. She forgot the fax — did not read it until Benjy called her, shattering her busy schedule and her usual calm.)

When Benjy read it, he called 911, then hollered, "Marianne!" They ran together to the car, waiting then as Denver followed and got inside, silent.

Soon sirens wound through the morning air. An officer knocked on the door at Martha's house. When no answer came, he tried the knob. It was unlocked.

Inside, the house was dark, hot, and smelly. Benjy, Marianne, and Denver arrived just after the officers.

"Wait here, Granddad. Please."

Walking in, Benjy saw his mother lying peacefully in bed, as if in sleep. Her hair had been combed. She wore a new nightdress that Bobbie had given her the day before. The covers were drawn neatly around her. The medicine bottles and drinking glasses had disappeared from beside the bed. A note pinned to the blanket said, "Dear Mother: In the name of love, you ruined my life. In the name of love, I am taking yours. Bobbie."

In shock, he turned and walked toward Bobbie's room. The computer was on—a screensaver depicting wild animals, leaping toward where his brother's body slumped over in the wheelchair.

Marianne took Benjy's hand. He turned, half-falling into her arms. She got Benjy through that day. Her mind raced ahead of his stunned one, to what had to be done. She turned down the thermostat, and spoke to the officers, who had called the coroner, and were making notes, moving about the house, asking questions.

"We need to call Sally and Victoria and Elizabeth. We must take your grandfather home."

With an officer, Marianne had gone to the computer, reached over Bobbie's body to tell the machine to print two copies. She handed one to the officer.

"Please do not give a copy of it to the press. Our sister is a congresswoman from California. The media will be interested." The officer looked up startled.

"The press could arrive at any time."

"I know the chief of police," Benjy said slowly. "I'll speak to him. No point in telling the local reporter about Sally. I'll call her."

A reporter came to the door. From the bedroom, Benjy and Marianne heard the questions being peppered at the officers.

"Other reporters will come. You need to be ready. They will ask every question, and when they find out about your sister—well, it could get a little crazy."

"Maybe we can avoid this one. Let's slip out the back door. We need to talk to our family."

Hurriedly, they left, going around the house, and got in the car. They were just shutting the doors when a reporter came running toward them. Marianne started the motor and backed out. A van approached from one of the television stations.

Marianne drove quickly away. "It feels like an invasion. I feel like we are exposing ourselves by leaving the house."

"We would be exposed being there as well." Benjy was more composed now. He held the fax in his hand, staring down at it, the words searing his brain.

They explained what they had found on the way to Denver's home, where they told Noreen. "N-no," she muttered.

"I have lived too long. I should have gone first," Denver's mind whirled unsettled. Those months after

Emma's death. He saw the fence, fallen, unable to take its place in the world of useful items, of connections, of people and things that held each other in an upright position. There had been snow next to the dilapidated fence, indicating a slough, the soil lacking adhesive qualities that would hold the wooden posts.

"Denver—don't you go thinkin' about yourself and all those other deaths. The family needs you again," Noreen had reminded him.

He did not respond at first. After a silence, he motioned to Benjy, "Come here." Benjy went. Denver sat in his old, favorite chair now and he lifted his thin arms to the younger man, pulling him toward him so Benjy went down on his knees as his grandfather took him in his arms. Both men began sobbing.

"You've done well, son. With the farm and your life. You're bound to feel bad about your mother and brother, but don't feel guilty."

"It's hard not to."

"Yes. None of us knew how to help them. Maybe we gave up, a little. It was the war, the wars—Harold, and Emma losing her heart over that, then Bobbie all cut up and Bryce gone. Martha wanted to protect and take care of her damaged child. You went to war but came back whole."

Benjy shook his head. Taking his arms away from his grandfather and sitting on the floor next to him, he said, "Nobody returns whole from war. Or innocent. It's the most horrible thing…but I guess it made me want, or appreciate, something clean and wholesome. I needed to shake the mud and the blood off."

"I want to lie down now." As Denver walked toward the bedroom, sorrow came at him like a hot, dry wind, like something that would not leave.

"Let me rest for a few minutes. Send Elizabeth in when she arrives. Sally, poor Sally. Victoria. Alice," Denver muttered.

"They do need you, and Sally will too when she arrives, and Victoria, but you don't need to do very much directly. They come to our home. The love you have given them, they share, even when you're not in the room. You need time and rest to come to terms with this." Noreen patted his hand.

"I don't want to come to terms with it."

"I know, but you need to remember, Denver. Remember and weigh all the good things that have happened and the good people that are in our family. There have been some crop failures, but the harvest has been plentiful."

The rest of that day was a blur to him. He had Noreen leave the bedroom door open and he heard part of what they said. Elizabeth came in and Denver held her as he had Benjy. And Victoria. Later—was it the same day or another?—he held Sally.

Benjy, Marianne, Elizabeth, Daniel, Alice and her family, and Victoria went to meet Sally at the airport, in part to shield her from the waiting media. The family circled her and moved forward down the long corridor. Video cameras ran. Microphones appeared before them.

"How do you feel? What do you think...?"

"The faceless many who always collect when any world is to be wrecked." Sally remembered a line from a poem by Auden and later repeated it to her grandparents. "Your home is my refuge." Sally sat in a rocking chair next to her grandfather's bed. Noreen sat on another chair. They drank hot peppermint tea. "The media follows me everywhere. My political enemies are trying to make something out of this. But never mind. We must make our own sense of it, or peace with it, or I don't know..."

Denver saw the deep circles under her eyes. Her face was puffy. Still, she was his success story and he needed to read it, wanting to find some balance in his mind for the failures and the sadness, the lives that had ended too early.

"First time I've ever been in one of these," Denver said. Benjy had a limousine pick them up for the service. Sally had warned the old couple that cameras would be in front of the mortuary. No media would be allowed inside. Benjy and his son, Denver, home from the military because of these deaths, and some friends provided a kind of barrier against intrusion as they made their way to the door.

Benjamin was standing awkwardly in the vestibule. Denver had not seen him in some time. Deep lines in his face had become folds, his dark hair had thinned, and his stomach protruded, reminding Denver of the saying, "He hasn't seen his feet in years." The two men shook hands. "You'll come over to Elizabeth's after the service?"

"Ah-h…maybe for a few minutes. Sorry I didn't call. Don't know what to say." Denver thought Benjamin needed a hat to work with, but not having one, his hands moved nervously and his gaze darted around.

"It's all right, Benjamin. We best get seated."

"Terrible thing, here," Benjamin needed forgiveness, perhaps, from Denver. Who was he to give such a thing? We do things and they have consequences, often unintended. Benjamin might have been different as a father.

Back then, Denver thought it his duty to provide food and clothing for his family, to "instruct them in the ways of the Lord," his father would have said, though he had not done that like his father had— holding the Bible as a kind of weapon against them.

"Honor Your Father and Mother," his father had roared. However, Denver respected his mother more than he did his father. What she did seemed worthy of his regard.

"Yes." Denver nodded absently and moved away. He was not quite ready to forgive Benjamin or to absolve him from responsibility for Bobbie who had grown up chasing footballs and girls and did not know what to do when the chase was over. Didn't Martha have some influence in those years? She had been cowed, Denver realized, by gratitude to Benjamin for "having her," when she had not felt herself worthy. And why was that? What had Emma and he done? He turned from questions he could not answer.

Those who knew Bobbie and Martha did their best to make some sense of what had happened, remembering good things about both of them. Victoria spoke of her father. Sally spoke of her mother: "She gave me wings, never telling me I couldn't do things because I was a girl. I remember one time we were driving somewhere in the car and I asked her if I could compete in a math contest. 'Of course, you can. You can do anything!' I don't know why she felt I could do things, but that she herself couldn't. She was quite successful when she worked, but Bobbie's injuries in Vietnam seemed to fall heavily on her. None of us is guilty for their deaths, but in some measure, perhaps, we all failed to reach and sustain them. If we learn anything from this, it should be to care for one another. It not only takes a village to raise a child. It takes a loving, supportive community of family and friends for any of us to live and laugh, to hold one another when holding is needed."

On January 5, 1998, the family celebrated Denver's 90th birthday with a quiet family gathering. Nothing else seemed appropriate.

Like Bobbie, and perhaps because of Bobbie and Martha's deaths, Denver had decided that it was time.

He lost desire of any kind. He did not have a stash
of pills—the coroner said Martha and Bobbie died of
overdoses—but he lost his appetite, eating only a bite
or two with Noreen's persuasion, sleeping most of the
time.

He slipped slowly away that January…often seeing Emma, holding her…mumbling that "the beets
need watering," or that he "must go out and milk
the cows." Sometimes he called out for "Harold…or
Bryce…or young Ronald."

The pasture was a full and a healthy green. The
corn was high. He was walking the ditch bank with
William. Sitting beside Emma, he was young again,
wanting to nestle into the folds of her. Sally and Bryce
were graduating. Bryce was alive and would always
be young. Elizabeth was greeting them at her front
door…and running forward to see the radio that he
had bought. The fence was standing tall. He was at
the Idaho State Fair with Noreen. Benjy and Bobbie
rode with him on the tractor. He was in his mother's
arms. The bright sunflower of Victoria bounced
through him.

It had snowed in the night. In the morning, the
sun sparkled against the whiteness that covered everything, extending in every direction…to the Owyhee
and Boise Mountains. Then everything was white,
gone, without sound.

The End

CPSIA information can be obtained
at www.ICGtesting.com
Printed in the USA
FSHW01n1537300518
48805FS

9 780970 373786